CATAMOUNT TRAIL
GUIDEBOOK

SEVENTH EDITION

Published by
Catamount Trail Association

1 Main Street, Suite 308
Burlington, VT 05401-5291
802-864-5794
www.catamounttrail.together.com
e-mail:ctamail@aol.com

Printed: August 1999

Catamount Trail Guidebook
Map Index

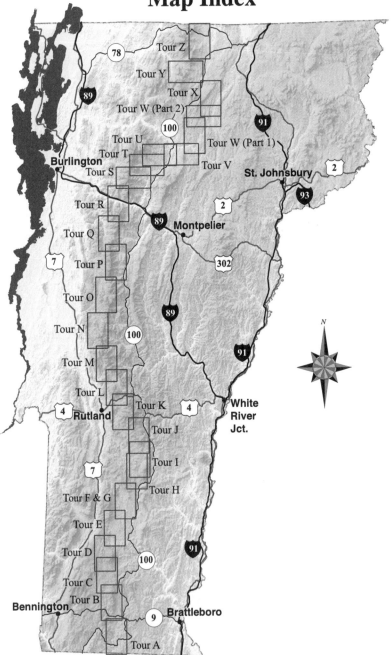

Tour Z

78

Tour Y

89

Tour X

Tour W (Part 2)

91

100

Tour U

Tour W (Part 1)

Tour T

Burlington

Tour V

Tour S

St. Johnsbury

2

93

Tour R

2

7

Tour Q

89 Montpelier

Tour P

302

Tour O

Tour N

100

89

Tour M

91

Tour L

Tour K

4

White River Jct.

4 Rutland

Tour J

7

Tour I

Tour F & G

Tour H

Tour E

Tour D

91

Tour C

100

Tour B

Bennington

9 Brattleboro

Tour A

N

Legend

Winter Trails

Catamount Trail Categories

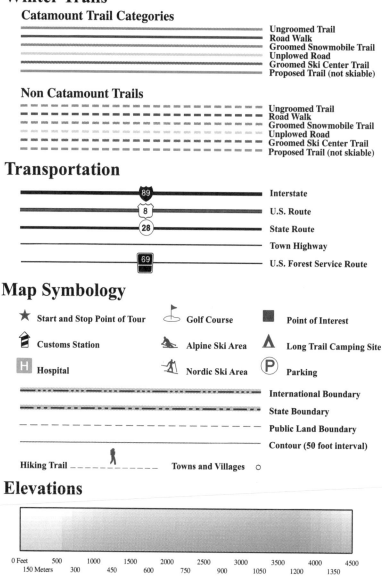

Ungroomed Trail
Road Walk
Groomed Snowmobile Trail
Unplowed Road
Groomed Ski Center Trail
Proposed Trail (not skiable)

Non Catamount Trails

Ungroomed Trail
Road Walk
Groomed Snowmobile Trail
Unplowed Road
Groomed Ski Center Trail
Proposed Trail (not skiable)

Transportation

89 Interstate

8 U.S. Route

28 State Route

Town Highway

69 U.S. Forest Service Route

Map Symbology

★ Start and Stop Point of Tour   ⚑ Golf Course   ■ Point of Interest

Customs Station   Alpine Ski Area   Ⓐ Long Trail Camping Site

H Hospital   Nordic Ski Area   Ⓟ Parking

International Boundary

State Boundary

Public Land Boundary

Contour (50 foot interval)

Hiking Trail _ _ _ _ _ _ _ _ _   Towns and Villages   ○

Elevations

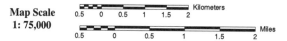

0 Feet	500	1000	1500	2000	2500	3000	3500	4000	4500
150 Meters	300	450	600	750	900	1050	1200	1350	

Map Scale

Map Scale
1: 75,000

Kilometers
0.5   0   0.5   1   1.5   2

Miles
0.5   0   0.5   1   1.5   2

Catamount Trail Guidebook

Original version published in 1985 by the Catamount Trail Association. Consecutive editions edited by Stephen Gladstone, Ray T. Auger, Pennie McEdward-Rand, and Rosemary V. Shea.

Cover: Watercolor and guache by Gardner Lane, Bolton VT
Cover Design: Harvest Moon Design, Williston, VT
Maps: Northern Cartographic, South Burlington, VT

Dedication

This edition of the Catamount Trail Guidebook is dedicated to all our members who have so happily and graciously donated their time, money and enthusiasm to build, maintain and support the Catamount Trail. Many thanks for your hard work clearing brush, your generous annual and trail fund gifts, your helpful trail reports, and your never ending support of the Trail. We hope you'll enjoy skiing it even more with this new guidebook!

Contents

Introduction 1

The Catamount Trail Association 1

How To Use the Guidebook 2

Catamount Trail Etiquette 3

Inn-to-Inn Skiing Along the Trail 4

Winter Camping Along the Trail 5

Suggested Day Touring Equipment 5

Tips for Skiers 7

Summer Use of the Catamount Trail 7

A Final Word 8

TOUR A: Massachusetts Border to Route 9 .... **12**

    Map A: Mass. Border to Medburyville Picnic Area (Rte. 9) 13

TOUR B: Route 9 to Somerset Reservoir **16**

    Map B: Route 9 to Somerset Reservoir 17

TOUR C: Somerset Reservoir to Kelley Stand Rd. **20**

    Map C: Somerset Reservoir to Kelley Stand Rd. 21

TOUR D: Kelley Stand Rd. to Kendall Farm Rd. **24**

    Map D: Kelley Stand Rd. to Kendall Farm Rd. 25

TOUR E: Kendall Farm Rd. to Route 11 .... **28**

    Map E: Kendall Farm Rd. to Route 11 29

TOUR F: Route 11 to Landgrove **30**

TOUR G: Landgrove to Greendale Parking Area **32**

    Map Tours F & G: Route 11 to Landgrove to Greendale 33

TOUR H: Greendale Parking Area to Healdville **36**

    Map H: Greendale Parking Area to Healdville 37

TOUR I: Healdville to Ninevah Four Corners **40**

    Map I: Healdville to Ninevah Four Corners 41

    Map J: Ninevah Four Corners to Tin Shanty 44

TOUR J: Ninevah Four Corners to Tin Shanty **45**

TOUR K: Tin Shanty to Route 4 .... **48**

    Map K: Tin Shanty to Route 4 49

TOUR L: Route 4 to Mountain Top **52**

Map L: Route 4 to Mountain Top 53

TOUR M: Mountain Top to Blueberry Hill **56**

Map M: Mountain Top to Blueberry Hill 57

TOUR N: Blueberry Hill to Natural Turnpike **60**

Map N: Blueberry Hill to Natural Turnpike 61

TOUR O: Natural Turnpike to Lincoln Gap **64**

Map O: Natural Turnpike to Lincoln Gap 65

TOUR P: Lincoln Gap to Mad River Barn **68**

Map P: Lincoln Gap to Mad River Barn 69

TOUR Q: Mad River Barn to Camels Hump Skiers Association **72**

Map Q: Mad River Barn to Camels Hump Skiers Association 73

TOUR R: Camels Hump Nordic Ski Center to Bolton Valley **76**

Map R: Camels Hump Nordic Ski Center to Bolton Valley 77

TOUR S: Bolton Valley Ski Center to Trapp Family Lodge **80**

Map S: Bolton Valley Ski Center to Trapp Family Lodge 81

TOUR T: Trapp Family Lodge to Edson Hill **84**

Map T: Trapp Family Lodge to Edson Hill 85

TOUR U: Edson Hill to Farm Resort **88**

Map U: Edson Hill to Farm Resort 89

TOUR V: Farm Resort to Route 15 .... **92**

Map V: Farm Resort to Route 15 93

TOUR W: Route 15 to Craftsbury Nordic Center **96**

Map W Part 1: Route 15 to Wiley Brook 97

Map W Part 2: Wiley Brook to Craftsbury Nordic Center 98

TOUR X: Craftsbury Nordic Center to Lowell General Store **102**

Map X: Craftsbury Nordic Center to Lowell General Store 103

TOUR Y: Lowell General Store to Hazen's Notch Nordic **106**

Map Y: Lowell General Store to Hazen's Notch Nordic 107

TOUR Z: Jay Pass to Canadian Border **110**

Map Z: Jay Pass to Canadian Border 111

Status of Individual Ski Tours 115

End-to-End Section Check-off List 116

INTRODUCTION

The Catamount Trail is a 300 mile cross-country ski trail running the length of Vermont. Starting in Readsboro on the Massachusetts border, it winds its way through the heart of the Green Mountains to North Troy on the Canadian Border. Along the route, the Trail passes several of Vermont's finest cross-country ski centers and many country inns and lodges.

The Trail is accessible to skiers of all abilities and runs along old logging roads, groomed cross-country ski center trails, snowmobile trails and public trails. The Trail offers skiers a unique opportunity for day-long tours or over-night inn-to-inn skiing. All tours offer a great way to experience the beauty of Vermont's mix of fields, hills and valleys.

The first Catamount Trail Guidebook was published in the form of a map in 1985. Each consecutive edition of the guidebook has reflected progress in the development of the Trail. With this edition, 92% of the Catamount Trail corridor is complete and open for skiing and snowshoeing. This edition incorporates all new Catamount routes and changes to existing routes as of August 1999. We thank all our members and volunteer Trail Chiefs for their help and feedback in making this guidebook as up-to-date and accurate as possible.

The goal of the Catamount Trail Association (CTA) is for people to use the Trail and experience the beauty and thrill of back-country skiing in Vermont. The Catamount Trail offers skiers some of the most unique skiing experiences to be found anywhere. Skiers of all abilities and interests will find skiing the Trail to be a rewarding and enjoyable experience. All of us involved with the Cata-mount Trail are proud of what we have created. We hope others get an opportu-nity to experience the Trail and share the joys of skiing and snowshoeing.

THE CATAMOUNT TRAIL ASSOCIATION

Mission and Organizational Structure

The Catamount Trail Association (CTA) is a volunteer nonprofit organiza-tion dedicated to building, promoting and protecting the Catamount Trail, Vermont's end-to-end cross-country ski trail, and to promoting cross-country skiing. The Association is guided by its Board of Directors. The staff consists of two co-executive directors, a land protection coordinator and a full-time executive assistant. At present, the Association consists of 1700 supporters who come from Vermont, New England, the greater U.S., and Canada.

History

The Catamount Trail began as an idea in the minds of three young Vermont men: Steve Bushey, Paul Jarris and Ben Rose. Steve Bushey, then a University of Vermont student in geography, researched the route and obtained access

1

privileges from various landowners as a thesis project. Steve, with friends Paul and Ben, skied the route on the first End-to-End Tour in 1984, and the Catamount Trail was born. The Association was incorporated in 1984 with the purpose of developing, administering and maintaining the Catamount Trail as a public resource.

Since then, with the help of many volunteers, great strides towards finishing the Trail have been made as well as initial steps to protect it. As of this printing, the Catamount Trail is about 92% complete.

Membership

We invite you to join the Catamount Trail Association. Skiers join the CTA in order to support the development and maintenance of the Catamount Trail. CTA members enjoy many benefits including: the Catamount Trail News, a discount on CTA publications and merchandise, a membership card good for half price skiing at most Vermont Touring Centers, and participation in most tours along the Trail. We hope you will join us in our efforts to create this invaluable recreational resource.

To join the CTA, fill out the form inserted in this book and return it to the CTA along with your check for the proper sum.

Events

Every year, the CTA hosts guided tours and other events along the Trail. Such events may be day-long tours, inn-to-inn tours, races, sugar house tours or Fall trail work days. For further information on the CTA events or to join us in building the Trail, please contact us or check our website at www.catamounttrail.together.com.

Publications and Information Available

Besides the Catamount Trail Guidebook, the CTA also publishes brochures on inn-to-inn skiing and cross-country touring centers along the Trail. The CTA is also happy to provide information and trail updates to anyone planning a ski tour or an end-to-end trip along the Catamount Trail.

HOW TO USE THIS GUIDEBOOK

This Guidebook breaks the Trail into twenty-six individual tours, each skiable in a single day. We suggest that you take your Guidebook and perhaps a compass with you when you ski the Catamount Trail. The Trail is marked with blue, plastic, diamond-shaped blazes imprinted with a black paw print. You should be able to find your way fairly easily. However, blazes do come down accidentally, and there are some spots where you might need to refer to your Guidebook.

This information is provided for sections of the Trail which are cut, blazed and officially open to the public. If a section of trail is not completely cut, blazed or does not have full landowner approval, then it is not included in the Guidebook.

In some places, the Catamount Trail follows segments of the VAST snowmobile trails. Many of these are temporary routes that we will use until we develop better skiing alternatives. On some of these sections, there are no CTA blazes, so you will want to have your Guidebook directions with you.

The CTA has worked long and hard to update the information included here, but undoubtedly, some errors do exist. If you discover any errors or discrepancies, please inform the CTA office. It is largely through your feedback that the Guidebook can be improved.

Difficulty Level

In choosing a tour, please realize that all the tours are not necessarily appropriate for you or your group. Do consider the group's physical fitness, back-country skiing experience, equipment, skiing skills, and familiarity with the route. We have included information to help you choose a tour for your ability level. All people who ski the Catamount Trail should feel comfortable negotiating a turn while on a moderate downhill, and should be physically fit enough to spend a minimum of four hours skiing in the cold. Remember that weather and snow conditions can change the difficulty of the tour drastically. Breaking trail through two feet of powder can double the normal time for a tour. The difficulty of the terrain, weather and snow conditions, skier's ability and familiarity with the route should all be considered in choosing a tour.

If you have any doubts, feel free to call the office or contact one of the ski centers in the area of the tour. **Remember, this is a wilderness ski trail.** While every effort has been made to remove hazards from the trail, some may still exist on the route. Skiers need to take personal responsibility for having a safe and enjoyable ski tour.

CATAMOUNT TRAIL ETIQUETTE

Private Landowners

Currently 60% of the Catamount Trail crosses private land. The CTA has permission to cross these lands due to the cooperation of these landowners. Continued access to these lands depends upon the continued good relations between skiers and landowners. Please respect the rights of landowners and stay on the blazed route. In addition, keep your dog on the trail with a leash and carry out any trash that you make or see. If you run into any problems, please let us know.

Ski Touring Center Trails

When you enter the trail system of a cross-country ski center, please check in at the center. Skiing the Catamount Trail does not exempt you from paying a trail fee at the center. Each center has its own policy; some will allow you to ski free, others may charge a fee. Bring along your CTA membership card to get a discount if you have to pay a fee. Whatever the policy, please cooperate with the center. Also note that most touring centers do not allow dogs on their trails, so plan your trip accordingly if bringing a canine friend along.

Snowmobile Trails

The Catamount Trail uses many snowmobile trails through the generosity of the Vermont Association of Snow Travelers (VAST). Skiers should step off the trail to allow snowmobiles to pass. VAST membership dues pay for the maintenance of these trails. If you will be skiing sections of the Catamount Trail which use parts of the VAST trails, please support the maintenance of these segments by joining VAST. Contact VAST at: P.O. Box 839, Montpelier, VT, 05601, 802-229-0005.

INN-TO-INN SKIING ALONG THE TRAIL

There are many country inns and bed and breakfasts along or near the trail. What could be better than enjoying a good meal and relaxed Vermont hospitality after a great day of skiing the Catamount Trail? In many cases, all you need to carry with you are clothes, toiletries, lunch and touring items. In some cases, an inn will transport your luggage to the next stop for you. The Catamount Trail Association has a number of brochures which can help you plan an inn-to-inn skiing trip along the Catamount Trail. Please call the CTA office for any of these free brochures.

The following establishments participate in our Inn-to-Inn Brochure series:

Killington Area Brochure-
Blueberry Hill Inn, Goshen, 800-448-0707
Chipman Inn, Ripton, 800-890-2390
Churchill House Inn, Brandon, 802-247-3078
Cortina Inn, Killington, 800-451-6108
Country Inns Along the Trail, Brandon, 800-838-3301
Edelweiss Motel, Killington, 800-479-2863
Inn at the Long Trail, Killington, 802-775-7181
Judith's Garden, Goshen, 802-247-4707
Mendon Mountainview, Killington, 802-773-4311
Mountain Top Inn, Chittenden, 802-483-2311
Pico Condos at Killington, 800-343-0762

Bolton, Morrisville and Stowe Area Brochure-
　　Anderson Lodge, Stowe, 800-336-7336
　　Bolton Resort, Bolton, 802-434-3444
　　Edson Hill Manor, Stowe, 800-621-0284
　　Farm Resort, Morrisville, 800-822-4353
　　Fiddlers Green Inn, Stowe, 800-882-5346
　　The Gables Inn, Stowe, 802-253-7730
　　Golden Eagle Resort, Stowe, 800-626-1010
　　The Inn at Turner Mill, Stowe, 800-992-0016
　　Mount Mansfield Youth Hostel, Stowe, 802-253-4010
　　Ski Inn, Stowe, 802-253-4050
　　Stowehof Inn and Resort, Stowe, 800-932-7136
　　Topnotch, Stowe, 800-451-8686
　　Trapp Family Lodge, Stowe, 800-826-7000

Northeast Kingdom Area Brochure-
　　Brassknocker Bed & Breakfast, Craftsbury, 802-586-2814
　　Craftsbury B&B on Wylie Hill, Craftsbury Common, 802-586-2206
　　Craftsbury Outdoor Center, Craftsbury Common, 800-729-7751
　　Golden Maple Inn, Wolcott, 800-639-5234
　　Highland Lodge, Greensboro, 802-533-2647
　　Inn on the Common, Craftsbury Common, 800-521-2233
　　Lakeview Inn, Greensboro, 802-533-2291
　　Village House Inn, Albany, 802-755-6722

WINTER CAMPING ALONG THE TRAIL

　　Because most of the Catamount Trail is on private land, camping is not allowed along most of the Catamount Trail. It is possible to winter camp in some areas in the Green Mt. National Forest. For information, contact:

Green Mountain National Forest
231 North Main St.
Rutland, VT, 05701
802-747-6700

SUGGESTED DAY TOURING EQUIPMENT

　　Below is a list of things you should think about bringing on a tour. One never knows what may happen on a ski tour, especially when you may be miles away from any access point. Be prepared! Basically, your pack should include items from a number of different categories:

First aid and emergencies: What will you do if you or someone in your party gets hurt and you are miles away from any access point? Bring a first aid kit and more importantly, clothes, food and other aids to ward off hypothermia. Be prepared by knowing where the access points along the trail are located and how to get help.

Ski and pole repair: An easy, fun tour can turn into a marathon adventure when your equipment breaks. First and foremost, be sure your equipment is in good working order before you start your tour. Next, bring ski repair items (extra binding bail, screws, and pole basket) that can fix your type of skis and poles. Someone else may not have anything that can fix your particular type of equipment.

Environment: Be prepared for all types of weather. Listen to the weather forecast before going on the tour. Take plenty of warm clothes and always dress in layers. You may be hot and sweaty in the morning, but the wind may pick up and the temperature drop 20 degrees by the afternoon. Also be prepared to deal with darkness should your tour take longer than expected.

Food and Water: You should expect to eat & drink almost twice as much on a tour day than you normally do. Bring lots of food and a good supply of liquids. Water bottles often freeze during a winter day tour so bring a thermos as well. Even if you don't eat all your food, someone else may be forever grateful for that extra brownie that got him/her across the last mile of Trail.

Sample Day Touring Equipment List

Guidebook
appropriate skis, boots & poles
day pack
lots of clothing layers
water &/or thermos of hot drink
hearty lunch and snacks
warm mittens, liners & spare pair
extra wool hat
outer wind shell (rain shell if it's likely)
extra dry socks
head lamp
ski wax, cork & scraper

climbing skins
first aid kit (& moleskin)
camera
duct tape
spare ski tip
spare pole basket
space blanket
picture wire
multipurpose tool
sunglasses
matches

TIPS FOR SKIERS

* Use appropriate equipment for the tour. In many cases, basic touring skis, poles, and comfortable boots are suitable. On more difficult sections, and especially if the trail is hard packed or icy, steel edges and skins may be more appropriate.

* Always carry basic first aid supplies, extra warm clothing and plenty of food and water.

* Always carry a repair kit to fix skis, bindings and poles that could break.

* Before you go, familiarize yourself with any possible exit points. If your group has an extra car, it s a good idea to leave one at a midway exit point in case some skiers want to stop early.

* Let someone know where you are going and when you should be back.

* Be aware of weather conditions and the time of day. The weather changes quickly in the mountains. It also gets cold and dark very early.

*In general, use good judgment. The guidebook is an aid, not a substitute for good common sense. Be willing to turn back if circumstances call for abandoning a tour.

SUMMER USE OF THE CATAMOUNT TRAIL

The Catamount Trail is a winter-use only trail. Much of the Trail crosses privately owned lands. These landowners give the CTA permission to cross their lands during the winter only for cross-country skiing and snowshoeing. Please respect these landowners wishes and stay off their land in the non-snow seasons. Failure to do this could cause landowners to close their land to public use and endanger the Catamount Trail.

If you would like to use a particular section of the Trail in the non-snow months, please contact the landowners and ask their permission. There are also sections of the Catamount Trail that are parts of other summer-use trail systems. It is fine to use these sections of Catamount Trail in the summer under the administering organization s guidelines. Educating yourself on where you are and respecting the wishes of the parties involved will greatly benefit the existence and promotion of the Catamount Trail.

A FINAL WORD

In the end it is most important that you get out and enjoy cross-country skiing and the beautiful, natural, winter scenery of Vermont. So wax up your skis, lace up your boots and go skiing on the Catamount Trail!

CTA Members celebrate ten years of building the Trail with the Tenth Anniversary Ski Tour at the Trapp Family Lodge in Stowe, VT.   *CTA file photo.*

Catamount Trail

Ski Tour Descriptions
&
Maps

DAY SKI TOUR A:
MASSACHUSETTS BORDER TO ROUTE 9

TOUR PROFILE:

TOUR SNAPSHOT: One of the easiest sections, mostly ungroomed, and runs along the scenic Deerfield River, Harriman Dam and Harriman Reservoir.

LODGING: Whitingham Farm B&B, Whitingham, 800-310-2010

START POINT: Harriman Station (MA Border)- to get to the Border you must park at the Harriman Station and ski south.

FINISH POINT: Medburyville (Rte. 9)

TOTAL MILEAGE: 15.0

DIFFICULTY OF TOUR: Easy intermediate. Easy access points on trail.

ACCESS/EXIT POINTS:
1. Harriman Station
2. Rte. 100, 0.7 miles east of power plant.
3. Harriman Dam Parking Area (at foot of reservoir)
4. Medburyville

DIRECTIONS: **To Mass. Border and Harriman Station:** Take Route 100 north from Readsboro over the bridge, and turn right (south). To ski to Harriman Station, bear left just south of the houses and park. This is the south end of the road walk- the Trail south starts on an old road. To drive to Harriman Station, head straight instead of bearing left and follow the

Map A: Mass. Border to Medburyville Picnic Area (Rte. 9)

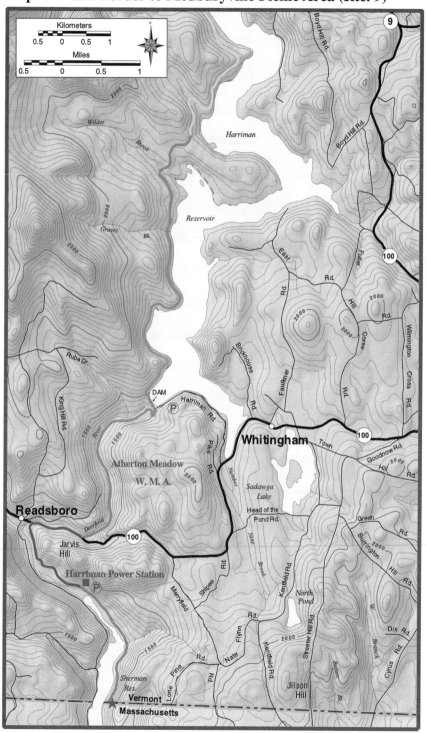

road to its end.

To Harriman Dam: Harriman Road is on the north side of Route 100- your first left if coming from Readsboro or your second right if coming from Whitingham. Park in the lot at the end of the road.

To Medburyville: Take Rte. 9 about 3 miles west of Wilmington. Turn left and go over the bridge to the village. Turn left after crossing bridge and drive to picnic area.

NOTE: Harriman Station and Harriman Dam are two different places. There are two Harriman Roads: one to the station, one to the dam (see map).

DISTANCE TO MAJOR LANDMARKS:

Start	Finish	Mileage	Total
Harriman Station	MA Border	1.5	1.5
MA Border	Harriman Station	1.5	3.0
Harriman Station	Start road walk	1.0	4.0
Start road walk	Rte. 100	0.3	4.3
Rte. 100	Start skiing	0.7	5.0
Ski point	Harriman Dam Parking	3.0	8.0
Parking Area	Graves Brook	3.0	11.0
Graves Brook	End of plowing	4.0	15.0

ROUTE DESCRIPTION:

From the parking lot at Harriman Station, follow the road south to a gate. To reach the border you must ski south on the Trail 1.5 miles to a granite marker on the river side of the Trail (1.5).

Heading north, from the border, the Catamount Trail follows an old railroad bed along the east side of the Deerfield River. Just before Harriman Station, watch for a turn to the right and follow the old railroad bed above the station. The Trail crosses Harriman Road twice, ending at the south end of the road walk (see directions) (2.5). The walk takes you east along Rte. 100 to a white house and a green house side by side on the right. Just beyond the houses, the Trail bears off to the north (left) at power pole #513 (which has a CTA blaze on it) following an old railroad bed with the Deerfield River on the left (1.0).

The Trail soon crosses Tobey Brook, which may be difficult to cross in times of high water. Follow the railroad bed along the Deerfield River until you reach a power line clearing, and then follow a snowmobile trail up a steep slope for about 150 yards. (If southbound, the turnoff to the CT from the snowmobile trail under the powerlines is easy to miss, watch for blazes.) The Trail turns sharply left at the top of the climb, following a logging road for a short distance through the gate to the dam at the south end of Harriman Reservoir. There is a parking area (see directions) at the dam which is plowed for winter access (3.0). (To reach the dam you must remove your skis and walk through a narrow opening in the fence next to a maple tree in the parking lot.)

Crossing the dam, the Trail follows an old railroad bed up the west side of Harriman Reservoir. Initially it follows a snowmobile trail. After about 1 mile the CT heads straight at a four way junction leaving the snowmobile trail. It winds along the bank and crosses several streams including the Graves and Wilder Brooks. Both brooks have bridges for crossing (3.0). After crossing Wilder Brook (the second bridge) watch for the Trail turning right after about 100 yards. Rejoin the snowmobile trail and ski through the US Generating Corp. picnic area. Continue north on the old railroad bed until you reach the end of plowing in Medburyville (4.0). From the picnic area in Medburyville the Trail is incomplete to Rte. 9.

Howard Baker finds the stone marker at the Massachusetts/Vermont border.
Photo by Clem Holden.

DAY SKI TOUR B:
ROUTE 9 TO SOMERSET RESERVOIR

TOUR PROFILE:

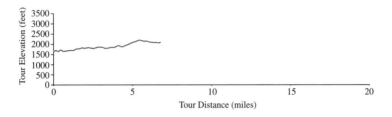

TOUR SNAPSHOT: A remote wilderness section with varied terrain offering views of the East Branch River, Mt. Snow, and Searsbourg Reservoir.

LODGING: Mt. Snow Valley Chamber of Commerce, 877-VT-SOUTH

START POINT: Rte. 9 (west of Wilmington)

FINISH POINT: Somerset Reservoir

TOTAL MILEAGE: 7.4

DIFFICULTY OF TOUR: Intermediate terrain. Generally flat with some very steep ascents and descents. Very remote with few access points, 100% ungroomed.

ACCESS/EXIT POINTS: 1. Deerfield River at Rte. 9
2. East Branch Trail
3. Somerset Dam Parking Lot

DIRECTIONS: **To Deerfield River at Rte. 9:** Approximately 4.5 miles west of Wilmington, shortly before reaching the bridge across the Deerfield River, look for Lind Well Drilling on the right side. The owner will usually let you park here if asked courteously. To get to the CT, walk west along Rte. 9 to the bridge (Deerfield River). The Trail heads north into the woods on an old road on the east bank of the river.

To East Branch Trail: Drive north on the

Map B: Route 9 to Somerset Reservoir

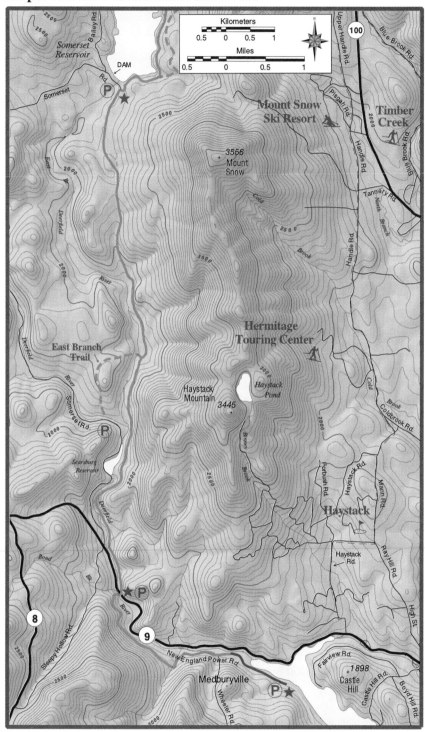

Somerset Dam Access Rd. for 2 miles. Locate a sign for NEPCO East Branch Trail on your right.

To Somerset Dam: Drive west of Wilmington approximately 5.0 miles. Turn right (north) onto the Somerset Dam Access Rd. Drive to the end (approximately 9 -10 miles) and park at the end of plowed road.

DISTANCE TO MAJOR LANDMARKS:

Start	Finish	Mileage	Total
Rte. 9	Vose Brook	0.5	0.5
Vose Brook	East Branch Trail	2.6	3.1
East Branch Trail	Road	3.8	6.9
Road	Parking Lot	0.5	7.4

ROUTE DESCRIPTION:

From Rte. 9 on the east side of the river, the Trail heads north on an old road. After about .75 miles, the road turns sharply to the right and heads uphill. At this turn, the Catamount Trail goes straight into the woods towards Vose Brook. Cross the brook on a bridge and then follow the old railroad bed. The Trail parallels the Deerfield River. After about 1 mile, you will see the Searsburg Dam spill-way. At this point, due to an old landslide, the Catamount Trail veers to the right and zig-zags up a steep hill. Once at the top of the hill, the Trail continues north and then descends in a north westerly direction. In about 0.3 miles, you will emerge from the woods to see the Searsburg Reservoir. The Trail now heads back into the woods, and climbs northeast uphill, then traverses for a stretch to a point where it makes a couple of switchbacks to get back down to the river and railroad bed. Here the Trail continues north, generally following the bank of the river on the old railroad bed. After passing the confluence of the Deerfield and East Branch Rivers, continue straight (north) for roughly half a mile. You will then cross a bridge and see the yellow blazed East Branch Trail joining the Catamount Trail from the left. This trail is your last possible exit/ access point for about 4.5 miles. It is about 0.5 miles from this junction out to the Somerset Access Rd. via the East Branch Trail.

To continue north on the Catamount Trail, just follow the blazes north crossing a couple of bridges along the way. These bridges were built by youths from the Vermont Youth Conservation Corps. The Trail eventually leaves the river. The ridge of Mt. Snow will be seen to the east along the way. After 4.5 miles, you will emerge on the road just below the Somerset Dam. Turn right and ski up the road to the parking lot.

BECOME A CATAMOUNT TRAIL END-TO-ENDER!

Skiers who ski each section of the 300 mile long Catamount Trail are awarded End-to-End Certificates and CTA pins. To become an official end-to-ender, you must record the date and condition of each section you ski in a journal. You need not ski all sections at once or in consecutive order. Just keep track of skied sections so that when you finish all twenty-six tours, you can submit your journal to get your certificate, pin and the special status that comes with being an end-to-ender!

DAY SKI TOUR C:
SOMERSET RESERVOIR TO KELLEY STAND ROAD

TOUR PROFILE:

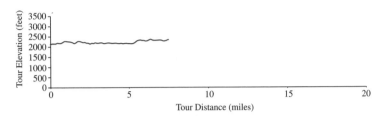

TOUR SNAPSHOT: An ungroomed wilderness section offering views of Somerset Reservoir and Grout Pond with connections to snowmobile trails for loop tour possibilities.

LODGING: • Winter Camping at Grout Pond Cabin (first come first serve), U.S. Forest Service, Manchester, 802-362-2307
• Stratton Mtn. Inn & Village Lodge, 800-777-1700

START POINT: Somerset Dam/Reservoir

FINISH POINT: Kelley Stand Road Parking Area

TOTAL MILEAGE: 7.7

DIFFICULTY OF TOUR: Easy-intermediate, but very remote. Access points only at the start and finish. 90% ungroomed.

ACCESS/EXIT POINTS: 1. Somerset Dam
2. Kelley Stand Road Parking Area

DIRECTIONS: **To Somerset Dam:** Drive west of Wilmington on Rte. 9 approximately 5 miles. Turn right (just after crossing the Deerfield River) onto the Somerset Dam Access Road. Drive 9-10 miles to the dam (end of plowing).

To Kelley Stand Road Parking Area: 6 miles west of Route 100 in West Wardsboro, on the Arlington/ West Wardsboro (Kelley Stand) Road.

Map C: Somerset Reservoir to Kelley Stand Road

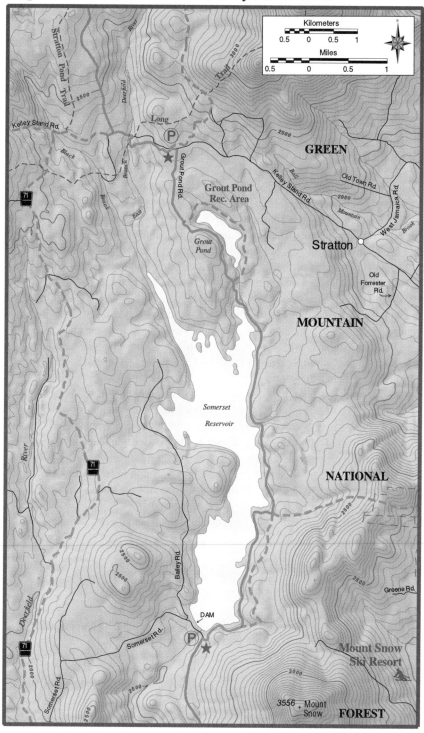

DISTANCE TO MAJOR LANDMARKS:

Start	Finish	Mileage	Total
Parking Lot	1st Bridge	0.2	0.2
1st Bridge	Moon Brook Bridge	2.0	2.2
Moon Brook Bridge	VAST Trail	0.5	2.7
VAST Trail	Grout Pond Picnic Area	4.0	6.7
Grout Pond Picnic Area	Kelley Stand Rd.	1.0	7.7

ROUTE DESCRIPTION:

From the Somerset Dam parking lot, cross the snowmobile trail and head north into the woods by the lake. Soon after entering the woods, you will cross a small plank bridge followed by a larger bridge which you may need to take your skis off to cross because of the steps. The Trail then runs along the lake shore for three miles, sometimes making short detours into the woods to avoid rough ground. You will get nice views of the lake at various points along the way. After crossing a large bridge at Moon Brook, continue on for about one more mile. At this point you will reach an intersection with a trail that is sometimes used by snowmobiles. The Catamount Trail crosses this trail and continues on along the reservoir. (Turning left on this trail will take you down to the reservoir, turning right on this trail will take you to a large groomed VAST snowmobile trail. You can turn right on the VAST trail to loop back to the Somerset Dam Parking Area.) Views of Stratton Mt. to the north and Mt. Snow to the south can be seen at various points along the way.

As you approach Grout Pond, other trail networks will intersect the Catamount Trail. The Grout Pond trails are marked with plain blue diamonds. Be cautious about which blazes you are reading. Follow the Catamount Trail pawprint blazes. The Trail will traverse the west side of Grout Pond (which is visible through the trees if you look down to your right). The Trail emerges at the Grout Pond Picnic area where there is a cabin open year around for use on a first-come-first-serve basis. To get to Kelley Stand Road, follow the access road/snowmobile trail (approx. 1 mile) to where it meets Kelley Stand Road. The plowed parking lot is directly across from the Grout Pond entrance.

Grout Pond Recreation Area

Grout Pond is a US Forest Service Recreation Area featuring campsites, a winter camping cabin, and a small trail system. It is a great place for a day ski trip, especially late in the season when its deep snow accumulation can be appreciated. For more information and a map of the area, contact the US Forest Service at the Manchester Ranger District office at 2538 Depot St., Manchester Center, VT, 05255, 802-362-2307.

DAY SKI TOUR D:
KELLEY STAND RD TO KENDALL FARM RD

TOUR PROFILE:

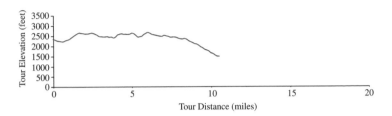

TOUR SNAPSHOT: A primarily backcountry section in the Green Mountain National Forest connecting to many snowmobile trails and Stratton Pond.

LODGING:
- Red Fox Inn, Bondville, 802-297-2488
- Stratton Mtn. Inn & Village Lodge, 800-777-1700

START POINT: Kelley Stand Road Parking Area

FINISH POINT: Kendall Farm Road (off Rte. 30)

TOTAL MILEAGE: 10.25

DIFFICULTY OF TOUR: Easy to intermediate, pleasant and scenic; long but ending with a downhill run. 95% ungroomed.

ACCESS/EXIT POINTS:
1. Kelley Stand Road
2. Kendall Farm Road

DIRECTIONS: **To Kelley Stand Road:** 6 miles west of Route 100 in West Wardsboro, on the Arlington/West Wardsboro (Kelley Stand) Road.

To Kendall Farm Road: Located on the south side of Rte. 30 approximately 6.5 miles south of Rte. 11 & 30 intersection or 1 mile north of Bondville. Travel 2.2 miles on Kendall Farm Rd. to the end of plowing.

Map D: Kelley Stand Rd. to Kendall Farm Rd.

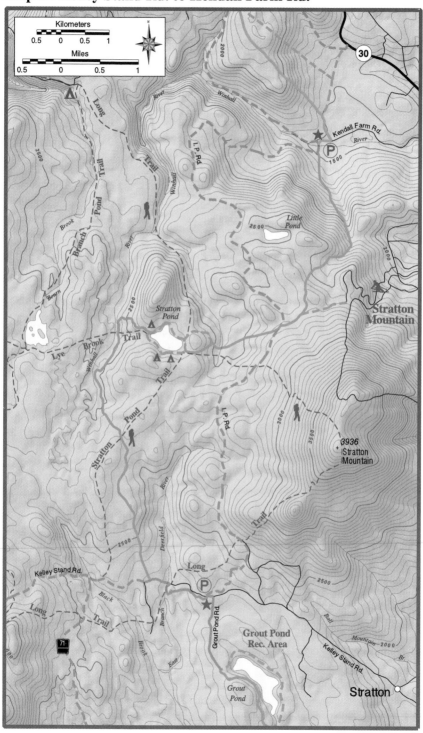

DISTANCE TO MAJOR LANDMARKS:

Start	Finish	Mileage	Total
Kelley Stand Rd	Trailhead	1.0	1.0
Trailhead	Fork in Trail	0.9	1.9
Fork in Trail	Stratton Pond Trail	1.1	3.0
Stratton Pond Trail	Footbridge	1.7	4.7
Footbridge	Turn	0.2	4.9
Turn	Stratton Pond-NW End	0.4	5.3
Pond-East End	Stream Crossing	1.0	6.3
Stream Crossing	I.P. Road	1.0	7.3
I.P. Road	Dead Horse Hill Trail	0.1	7.4
D.H.H.T./ I.P. Road	Log Landing	2.75	10.15
Log Landing	Kendall Farm Rd.	0.1	10.25

ROUTE DESCRIPTION:

From the Kelley Stand Road Parking Area, follow the Kelley Stand Road west and downhill, for 0.75 miles past the old parking area (wide spot in the road) at the East Branch Brook. Go uphill for 0.25 miles and at the point where the hill levels off, the Trail leaves Kelley Stand Road and goes north (right) following a logging road (1.0). The trail markers begin at this point.

The Trail follows the logging road to a fork (0.9), the right fork of which is a dead end. Taking the left fork, the Trail follows a wide logging road and crosses the Stratton Pond Trail, marked with blue paint (1.1). A short distance past the S.P. Trail, the Catamount Trail becomes a narrow path. The Trail reaches a wooden footbridge (1.7). Just before the bridge, the Lye Brook Trail joins from the left. This blue paint-blazed trail leaves to the right just after crossing the bridge. The Catamount Trail continues straight ahead along the edge of a beaver meadow before making a sharp right turn and heading east up a wooded hillside. After the terrain levels off, the Trail ends up near the former site of the Stratton View Shelter on the north side of Stratton Pond (0.4). The trail markers end here, and resume where the Trail continues east of the pond (0.4). There will soon be a route cut and marked following the southern edge of the pond. Until then, follow the hiking trail along either shoreline to the east side of the pond.

About 100 yards north of a clearing at the eastern end of Stratton Pond, the Catamount Trail follows the Long Trail east for about 100 feet. It then follows a winding logging road heading generally east. The logging road traverses a wooded hillside, then descends to a stream crossing (1.0). After crossing another stream it ascends a hill. After the hill levels off, it crosses a wide, well-maintained logging road and snowmobile trail known as the I.P. (International Paper) Road (1.0).

(Stratton Mountain Resort can be reached by crossing the I.P. Road and following the logging road further for about 1 mile. Just before the logging road swings to the left at the West Ridge Circle Road turnaround, bushwack about

100 yards east to the "Wanderer" downhill ski trail.)

The Catamount Trail goes straight across the I.P. Road, follows a secondary snowmobile trail for 400 yards and then bears left onto the Dead Horse Hill Trail, a primitive snowmobile trail. It follows this trail downhill to the north and in 2.75 miles comes out to a log landing . Here you turn right to join the I.P. Road again. The C.T. continues north over a wooden vehicle bridge and reaches the end of Kendall Farm Road after about 100 yards. The blazing ends here at Kendall Farm Rd.

Partners

About forty percent of the Catamount Trail lies on public lands managed by the US Forest Service and the VT Department of Forests, Parks, and Recreation. The CTA works with both these agencies to manage and maintain the Catamount Trail on these lands.

DAY SKI TOUR E:
KENDALL FARM RD TO ROUTE 11

This section is currently incomplete. The CTA hopes to have this section open for the 2000/01 season. Please call the CTA office for an update on status if you would like to ski this section.

TOUR PROFILE (for proposed route):

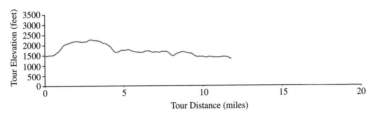

LODGING:
- See Lodging for Tour D
- Wiley Inn, Peru, 888-843-6600
- Johnny Seesaw's, Peru, 800-424-CSAW
- Manchester Highlands Inn, Manchester, 800-743-4565
- Meadowbrook Inn, Peru, 800-498-6445

START POINT: Kendall Farm Rd.

FINISH POINT: Rte. 11 (Meadowbrook Inn)

All Trail updates are published in the Catamount Trail News and are also posted on our website at www.catamounttrail.together.com.

Map E: Kendall Farm Rd. to Route 11

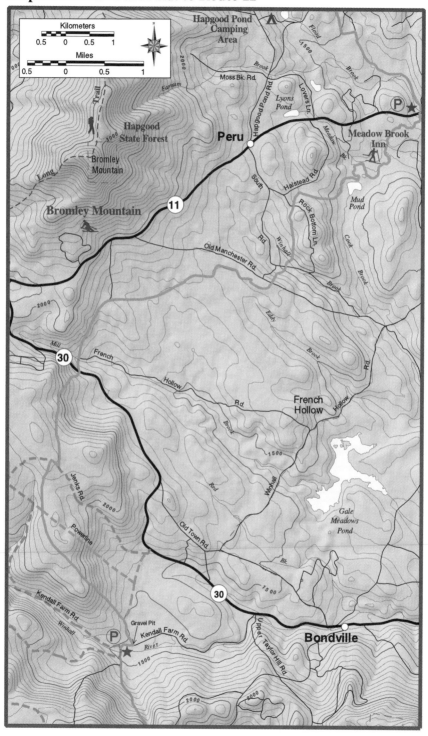

DAY SKI TOUR F:
ROUTE 11 TO LANDGROVE

This section is currently closed and being re-routed onto Forest Service land. The CTA hopes to have this section approved and open by 2000/01. Please call the office for updates on status if you would like to ski this section.

TOUR PROFILE: See Tour G.

LODGING:
- Meadowbrook Inn, Landgrove, 800-498-6445
- Landgrove Inn, Landgrove, 800-669-8466
- Londonderry Inn, So. Londonderry, 802-824-5226

START POINT: Rte. 11 (Meadowbrook Inn)

FINISH POINT: Junction of Little Michigan Rd. (FSR 12) and Danby-Mt. Tabor Rd. (FSR 10) in Landgrove.

Skiers step off the Trail to let a dog sled go by on the Mt. Tabor Road segment of the Landgrove to Greendale tour.

DAY SKI TOUR G:
LANDGROVE TO GREENDALE PARKING AREA

TOUR PROFILE (tours F & G):

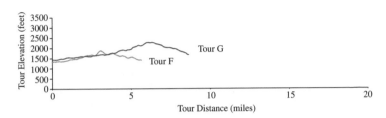

TOUR SNAPSHOT:	A part back-country, part snowmobile trail section running through lovely sections of the Green Mountain National Forest and ending with a long downhill run on the Jenny Coolidge Brook Trail.
LODGING:	• See Lodging for Tour F • The Darling Family Inn, Weston, 802-824-3223 • The Inn at Weston, 802-824-6789 • The Wilder Inn, Weston, 802-824-8172
START POINT:	Junction of Little Michigan Rd. (FSR 12) and Danby-Mt. Tabor Rd. (FSR 10) in Landgrove.
FINISH POINT:	Greendale Winter Parking Area (FSR 18 & FSR 17 Jct.)
TOTAL MILEAGE:	9.5
DIFFICULTY OF TOUR:	Intermediate with some difficult sections. Many exit points and alternate trail possibilities.
ACCESS/EXIT POINTS:	1. End of plowing on Danby-Mt. Tabor Rd (FSR 10) 2. Moses Pond Road (FSR 29) 3. Greendale Winter Parking Area
DIRECTIONS:	**To Danby-Mt. Tabor Rd. (FSR 10):** From Weston: From the Weston Post Office on Route 100 take the Landgrove-Weston Rd. west 4.2 miles to Little Michigan Rd. Go right on Little Michigan and travel 0.4 miles to Danby-Mt. Tabor Rd.

Map Tours F & G: Route 11 to Landgrove to Greendale

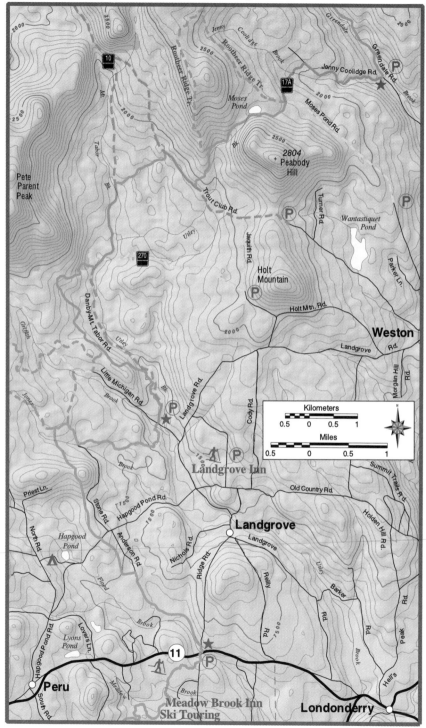

From Londonderry: From the junction of Rte. 100 N and Rte. 11, head west 0.5 miles on Routes 100 and 11 to where routes divide; stay on Rte. 11 another 0.4 miles to Landgrove Rd. Go right on Landrove Rd. (follow signs for Landgrove Inn) and travel 3.9 miles to Little Michigan Rd. (0.2 miles beyond Landgrove Inn). Left on Little Michigan Rd. and go 0.4 miles to Danby-Mt. Tabor Rd.

To Greendale Winter Parking Area: Take the Greendale Road off Rte. 100 1.9 miles north of Weston and 1.6 miles south of the Rte. 100/155 intersection. Go 2 miles on the Greendale Rd. (FSR #18) to the parking area which is immediately past a small bridge.

DISTANCE TO MAJOR LANDMARKS:

Start	Finish	Mileage	Total
Jct. Little Michigan Rd and Danby-Mt. Tabor Rd.	Utley Brook Trail	0.3	0.3
Utley Brook Trail	Danby-Mt Tabor Rd.	3.1	3.4
Danby-Mt Tabor Rd.	FSR #321	1.2	4.6
FSR #321 (366 & 367)	Moses Pond Trail	1.2	5.8
Moses Pond Trail	Root Beer Ridge Trail	0.6	6.4
Root Beer Ridge Trail	FSR 17A	1.1	7.5
FSR 17A	FSR 17 (Jenny Coolidge Rd.)	0.6	8.1
FSR 17	Greendale Parking	1.4	9.5

ROUTE DESCRIPTION:

From the junction of Little Michigan Rd. and Danby-Mt. Tabor Rd. drive north on the Danby-Mt. Tabor Rd. 0.2 miles to end of plowing (normally) and plowed turnaround (sign). Park along the road.

Put on your skis and ski 100 yards up the unplowed road to the entrance to the Utley Brook Trail on the left . This trail parallels FSR #10 for a while in fairly level terrain and then begins an uphill climb through mature hardwoods to an intersection with the Little Michigan Trail (on the left) (1.4). Continue on the Utley Brook Trail with varied elevation changes to intersect with FSR #10 (Mt. Tabor Road) again (1.7). Since the Utley Brook Trail can be moderately difficult, especially if the snow conditions are poor, you may want to choose the option of staying on the Mt. Tabor Road (at the beginning of the Utley Brook Trail) for a distance of 2.2 miles to the same point where the Utley Brook Trail intersects Mt. Tabor Road at its northern end. In either case continue north on FSR #10 for 1.2 miles until you reach FSR #321 on the right. This relatively wide old logging road meanders northeast for 0.7 miles and then curves southeast for 0.3 miles to a junction on the left with the trail to Moses Pond (FSR #365). Take this left and follow the trail for its 2 miles. This trail rises in elevation considerably, eventually joins a section of the Root Beer Ridge Trail and passes on the south side of Moses Pond which can be seen through the trees. It then drops down to intersect at a right angle with Moses Pond Road (FSR #29). Turn left onto this forest road which immediately turns right and becomes FSR #17A. After 0.6 miles of a downhill run with glorious mountain views, FSR #17A meets the Jenny Coolidge Brook Trail (FSR #17) at a "T" junction. Turn right onto this trail and enjoy a wonderful downhill ski of 1.4 miles along the Jenny Coolidge Brook to the Greendale Parking Area.

Mountain Valley Trails Association

The Mountain Valley Trails Association maintains an extensive network of cross-country ski trails in this area of Green Mountain National Forest. For information on these trails, the MVTA, or how to get involved in its activites, contact the Londonderry Area Chamber of Commerce at (802) 824-8178.

DAY SKI TOUR H:
GREENDALE PARKING AREA TO HEALDVILLE

TOUR PROFILE:

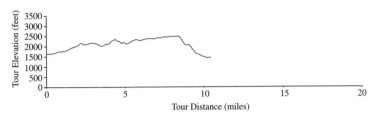

TOUR SNAPSHOT: This section travels over a groomed snowmobile route, and ungroomed trails through National and State Forests.

LODGING: See Lodging for Tour I

START POINT: Greendale Parking Area (FSR 18 & FSR 17 Jct.)

FINISH POINT: Healdville

TOTAL MILEAGE: 10.5

DIFFICULTY OF TOUR: Intermediate with several difficult sections.

ACCESS/EXIT POINTS: 1. Greendale Parking Area
2. Rte. 155
3. Healdville

DIRECTIONS: **To Greendale Parking Area:** Take the Greendale Road off Rte. 100 1.9 miles north of Weston and 1.6 miles south of the Rte. 100/155 intersection. Go 2 miles on the Greendale Rd. (FSR #18) to the parking area which is immediately past a small bridge.

To Healdville: Turn south off Rte. 103 onto Healdville Road 3.3 miles northwest of the Rte. 103- Rte. 100N junction (northwest of Ludlow). Follow Healdville Road 0.6 mi. to RR tracks. Immediately past tracks turn left (east) onto side road and park there. The Catamount Trail (and VAST Corridor #7) head south toward Greendale

Map H: Greendale Parking Area to Healdville

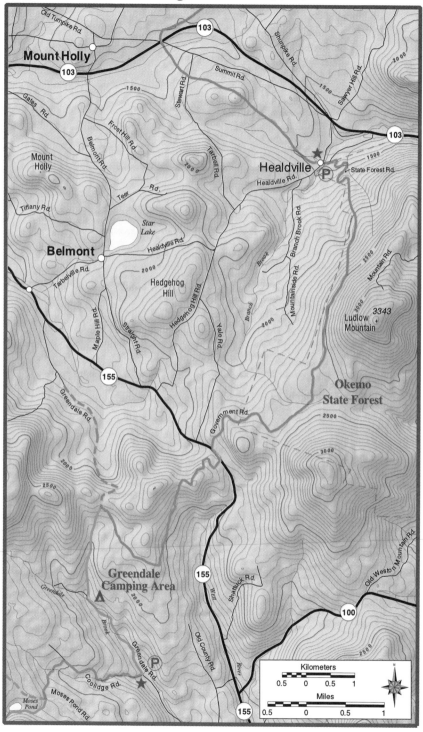

from the south side of the RR tracks just east of Healdville Road.

DISTANCE TO MAJOR LANDMARKS:

Start	Finish	Mileage	Total
Greendale Parking	Greendale Campground	1.0	1.0
Greendale Campground	Trail Fork-White Rocks R.A.	0.2	1.2
Trail Fork-White Rocks R.A	Trail Jct. VAST #7	1.2	2.4
Trail Jct. VAST #7	Rte. 155	2.8	5.2
Rte. 155	Okemo State Forest	0.7	5.9
Okemo State Forest	Healdville	4.6	10.5

ROUTE DESCRIPTION:

Head northwest from Greendale parking area on FSR #18. Approximately 0.2 miles past Greendale Camping Area (on left) go around gate with White Rocks Recreation Area sign. Ascend north-northeast up old logging road to a trail junction approximately 1.2 miles from White Rocks sign on right. The VAST Corridor #7 snowmobile trail joins the CT here and the two trails coincide for the rest of the tour. Turn right and follow the snowmobile trail 2.8 mi. to Rte. 155 and head north approximately 0.1 miles to a dirt road on the right which is the access road to Okemo State Forest (no sign). Travel in the described direction is mainly uphill. Head east on the access road approximately 0.1 miles to where VAST Corridor #7 currently enters on the left. Follow VAST #7 north through the State Forest to Healdville- approximately 5.3 miles. The last mile of this is steep with numerous sharp turns.

Lunch break on the Trail. *CTA file photo.*

DAY SKI TOUR I:
HEALDVILLE TO NINEVAH FOUR CORNERS

TOUR PROFILE:

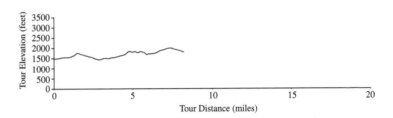

TOUR SNAPSHOT: Most of this route is shared with the groomed VAST Corridor 7 snowmobile trail.

LODGING:
- Echo Lake Inn, Tyson, 800-356-6844
- Inn at Water's Edge, Tyson, 888-706-9736

START POINT: Healdville

FINISH POINT: Ninevah Four Corners

TOTAL MILEAGE: 8.4

DIFFICULTY OF TOUR: Intermediate.

ACCESS/EXIT POINTS:
1. Healdville
2. Rte. 103
3. Ninevah Four Corners

DIRECTIONS: **To Healdville:** Turn south off Route 103 onto Healdville Road 3.3 miles northwest of the Route 103- Route 100N junction (northwest of Ludlow). Follow Healdville Road 0.6 miles to RR tracks. Immediately past tracks turn left (east) onto side road and park there. Catamount Trail (and VAST Corridor 7) head north toward Lake Ninevah from the west side of Healdville Road just south of the RR tracks.

To Ninevah Four Corners: Turn north off Route 103 onto Shunpike Road (just west of Harry's Cafe and Healdville Road) 3.4 miles

Map I: Healdville to Ninevah Four Corners

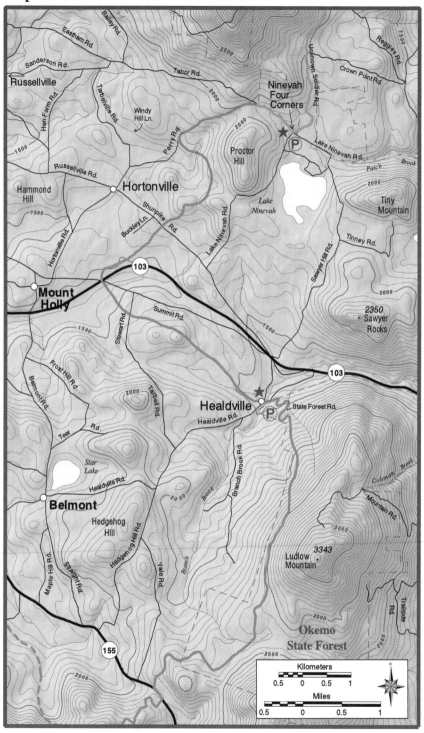

northwest of the Route 103 - Route 100N junction (northwest of Ludlow). Shunpike Road turns sharp left almost immediately- follow it 0.6 miles west to a fork in the road. Stay on Shunpike Road (right fork) another 0.7 miles to junction with Lake Ninevah Road. Turn right onto Lake Ninevah Road and follow it 2.0 miles to Ninevah Four Corners. Park on road. Catamount Trail south to Healdville heads west from Ninevah Four Corners on an unplowed road. CT north to Tin Shanty heads north from Ninevah Four Corners on a road that is sometimes plowed for a short distance.

NOTE: The road from Echo Lake on Route 100 to Lake Ninevah is not plowed in winter!

DISTANCE TO MAJOR LANDMARKS:

Start	Finish	Mileage	Total
Healdville	Rte. 103	4.0	4.0
Rte. 103	VAST Trail Jct.	3.9	7.9
VAST Trail Jct.	Ninevah Four Corners	0.5	8.4

ROUTE DESCRIPTION:

Follow VAST Corridor #7 N generally northwest approximately 4.0 miles to Rte. 103 crossing (5.9 miles west of junction of Rte. 103 and Rte. 100 N west of Ludlow). Continue to follow the VAST trail generally north-northeast approximately 3.9 miles until VAST Trail turns sharp left (north) off the old town road. Stay on the town road east (CT blazes) 0.5 miles to Ninevah Four Corners.

NOTE: Until a separate Catamount Trail route can be identified, possibly passing Lake Ninevah to the east, the Catamount Trail will follow VAST Corridor #7 from Healdville to where the VAST Trail turns North off the old town road approximately 0.5 miles west of Ninevah Four Corners. CTA members are urged to join VAST or one of its local clubs as a means of supporting this and other sections of the Catamount Trail maintained by VAST.

Vermont Association of Snow Travelers:
VAST

VAST is the nonprofit organization that maintains the Vermont state snowmobile trail system. CTA and VAST encourage skiers who ski on the snowmobile trails (including shared portions of the Catamount Trail) to join their local VAST club to support maintenance and grooming of these trails. To find out how to join, call the VAST central office at 802-229-0005.

Map J: Ninevah Four Corners to Tin Shanty

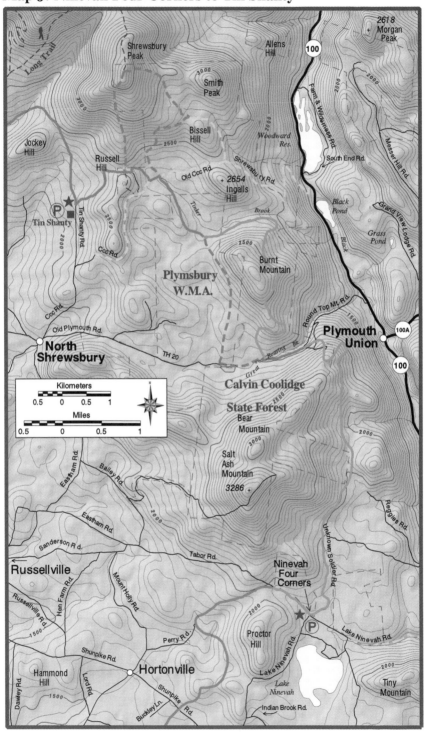

DAY SKI TOUR J:
NINEVAH FOUR CORNERS TO TIN SHANTY

TOUR PROFILE:

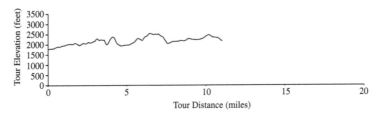

TOUR SNAPSHOT:
Mostly a wilderness tour running over Roundtop and Burnt Mountains through hardwood forest. Excellent views.

LODGING:
• Saltash Lodge, Plymouth Union, 802-672-3748
• Hawk Inn & Mtn. Resort, Plymouth, 800-685-HAWK

START POINT:
Ninevah Four Corners

FINISH POINT:
Tin Shanty off the CCC Road in North Shrewsbury

TOTAL MILEAGE:
11.8

DIFFICULTY OF TOUR:
Intermediate with several short difficult sections.

ACCESS/EXIT POINTS:
1. Ninevah Four Corners
2. Round Top Road in Plymouth Union
3. Tin Shanty

DIRECTIONS:
To Ninevah Four Corners: See Tour I

To Tin Shanty: From the former W.E. Pierce Grocery Store in North Shrewsbury take the CCC Road north 1.1 miles to a fork in the road. Take the left fork and continue north another 0.5 miles to a small house on left with a "Tin Shanty Camp" sign in the front window. Follow the unplowed road 0.3 miles north from Tin Shanty to a trail junction. The Catamount Trail (and VAST Corridor 7) both head north and south from this trail junction.

To Round Top Rd.: Round Top Road is on the west side of Route 100, 0.5 miles north of the junction of routes 100 and 100A in Plymouth Union, and 4.8 miles south of the junction of routes 100 and 4 in West Bridgewater. The junction of Round Top Road and unplowed Old Plymouth Road (see Route Description) is 0.9 miles west of Route 100 at a hairpin turn in Round Top Road.

NOTE: The CCC Road between Tin Shanty and Route 100 is not plowed in winter!

DISTANCE TO MAJOR LANDMARKS:

Start	Finish	Mileage	Total
Ninevah Four Corners	Flying Cloud Tr. Jct.	1.4	1.4
Flying Cloud	Round Top	2.4	3.8
Round Top	Great Roaring Brook	1.7	5.5
Great Roaring Brook	Flying Cloud Jct.	0.8	6.3
Flying Cloud Jct.	Log Landing	2.3	8.6
Log Landing	CCC Road	1.4	10.0
CCC Road	Tin Shanty Jct.	1.5	11.5
Tin Shanty Jct.	Tin Shanty	0.3	11.8

ROUTE DESCRIPTION:

From Ninevah Four Corners the Catamount Trail heads north up a dirt road (sometimes plowed for a short distance). The Trail passes a sand pit on the left (west) at 0.6 miles, then leaves the road left (west) at 1.1 miles. It crosses a brook (bridge) then shortly joins the Flying Cloud Trail - a blue blazed hiking trail - which it follows mostly north toward Round Top Mt - the site of the former Round Top Ski Area recently reopened as the Bear Creek Mountain Club. Near the top of Round Top, the Trail joins a snowmobile trail (Corridor 4) which it follows north then west over the summit, then northwest downhill (Caution - narrow and very steep in places!) to a junction with Old Plymouth Road. Go left (west) on Old Plymouth Road (if you head east you will reach Round Top Road, a good bailout point, in about 0.5 mile) to where it crosses Great Roaring Brook on a snowmobile bridge.

Just past the snowmobile bridge, the Trail turns sharp right and heads north uphill through an old clear cut. The Trail shortly enters woods on the right (east) side of the clear cut and soon joins a logging road which it follows until it rejoins the Flying Cloud trail on the southeast slope of Burnt Mountain. The Trail proceeds north on the east slope of Burnt Mt. (great views) and soon joins a logging road which it follows north and west to a log landing, then west to where it joins VAST corridor #7 which it follows north to the CCC Road on Grouse Hill North Road. Go west on the CCC Road 0.1 miles, then turn right (north) following VAST #7N 1.4 miles to a "T" junction. Turn left (south) to get to the Tin Shanty (0.3 miles). The Catamount Trail (and VAST Corridor #7) turns right and proceeds north toward Brewers Corner and Route 4 in Mendon.

Heading out on the Trail.   *CTA file photo*

DAY SKI TOUR K:
TIN SHANTY TO ROUTE 4

TOUR PROFILE:

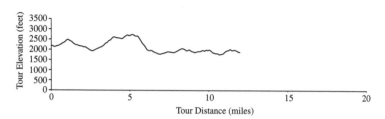

TOUR SNAPSHOT: This section follows a snowmobile route over Robinson Hill then continues as a remote backcountry ski through the Rutland City Forest. Mostly at an altitude of 2000' feet or more, good early/late snow can be expected.

LODGING:
- Rutland Region Chamber of Commerce, 800-756-8880
- The Inn at Rutland, 800-808-0575
- Cortina Inn, Killington, 800-451-6108

START POINT: Tin Shanty off the CCC Road in North Shrewsbury

FINISH POINT: Rte. 4 AT/LT/CT crossing just west of Pico

TOTAL MILEAGE: 12.0

DIFFICULTY OF TOUR: Intermediate to difficult. Steep downhill sections can be very difficult under some snow conditions.

ACCESS/EXIT POINTS:
1. Tin Shanty
2. Cold River Road
3. Brewers Corner
4. Rte. 4 AT/LT/CT Parking area

DIRECTIONS: **To Tin Shanty:** See Tour J.

To Brewers Corner: Turn onto the Wheelerville Road on the south side of Route 4, 4.1 miles west of Sherburne Pass. Brewers Corner is a right-angle turn in Wheelerville Rd. 4.0 miles south of Rte. 4. There is limited off-road parking. To reach

Map K: Tin Shanty to Route 4

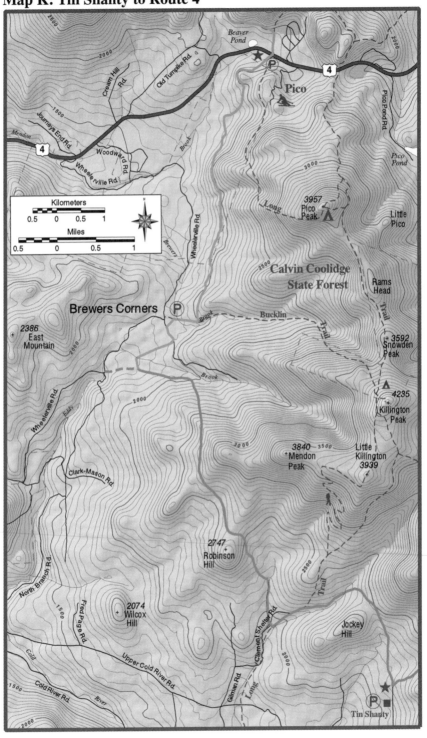

the Catamount Trail from Brewers Corner: if heading for Tin Shanty, go south on a logging road; if heading for Route 4, go east on the other logging road (also the Bucklin hiking trail).

To Rte. 4 AT/LT/CT Parking Area: The parking area is on the south side of Route 4, 0.9 miles west of Sherburne Pass. (This parking area also serves as an access for the Long Trail/ Appalachian Trail.)

DISTANCE TO MAJOR LANDMARKS:

Start	Finish	Mileage	Total
Tin Shanty	Catamount Tr./VAST #4 & #7	0.3	0.3
CT/VAST	Cold River Rd. Junction	2.7	3.0
Cold River Rd. Junction	Robinson Hill	1.5	4.5
Robinson Hill	Brewers Corner	3.5	8.0
Brewers Corner	Height of Land	3.5	11.5
Height of Land	Route 4	0.5	12.0

ROUTE DESCRIPTION:

Ski north 0.3 miles from Tin Shanty to reach the CT/VAST trail junction (signs). Continue north on the VAST snowmobile trail, then west around Jockey Hill. Reach junction with side trail to Cold River Road (possible exit point) at 3.0 miles. Turn right (north) and proceed generally north-northwest to the height of land east of Robinson Hill at 4.5 miles. From there the Trail descends toward Brewers Corner (possible exit point) which it bypasses by cutting across to the Bucklin Trail just before reaching Wheelerville Road at 8.0 miles. This is a good place to stop/begin a shorter tour. There is a small parking area where you may leave a car.

Head east on the Bucklin Trail and cross Brewers Brook (bridge). Shortly after, turn sharp left (north) and ascend an old logging road. From here the CT proceeds generally north through hardwood forest on a series of logging and skid roads connected by narrower winding trails. There are a number of brook crossings (some bridges) and much up and down although the route stays fairly close to 2,000 feet elevation. At approximately 11.0 miles, the CT turns sharp right (east) off the logging road and heads uphill on an old skid road to a height of land on a knoll which it circles. This is a nice scenic spot to enjoy a last snack and cup of tea before the long descent northeast to the AT/LT/CT parking area on Rte. 4.

When Landowners Share...
Show You Care

Roughly sixty percent of the Catamount Trail crosses land that is privately owned thanks to the generosity of about 200 landowners. This public use of private land is a privilege that can be threatened by inappropriate use of these lands.

"Show you care" by treating private land with the same respect you would want someone to treat your private property.

- Stay on designated trails
- Obey all posted signs
- Carry out what you carry in
- Keep dogs leashed or by your side
- Thank landowners you meet on the Trail for keeping their land open.

DAY SKI TOUR L:
ROUTE 4 TO MOUNTAIN TOP

TOUR PROFILE:

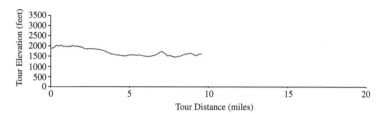

TOUR SNAPSHOT: This tour runs through ungroomed terrain, snowmobile trails, and the excellent groomed trails of Mt. Top Ski Center. It features fine views of Chittenden Reservoir.

LODGING:
• See Lodging Tour K
• Tulip Tree Inn, Chittenden, 800-707-0017

START POINT: Route 4 AT/LT/CT crossing just west of Pico

FINISH POINT: Mountain Top Ski Center

TOTAL MILEAGE: 9.7

DIFFICULTY OF TOUR: Intermediate

ACCESS/EXIT POINTS:
1. Route 4 AT/LT/CT Parking Area
2. Wildcat Road
3. Mountain Top Ski Center

DIRECTIONS: **To AT/LT/CT Parking Area:** See Tour K.

To Mountain Top Ski Center: Located on Mt. Top Road in Chittenden- look for signs.

To Wildcat Road: From Chittenden take the Dam Road east approximately 1.5 miles to a fork in the road. Take the right fork, Wildcat Road, and go 1.5 miles to the VAST/ CT trail junction on the left (north) side of the road. (A VAST signboard will be on the south side.) The CT/VAST Trails head southeast, then south, from there on Wildcat Road

Map L: Route 4 to Mountain Top

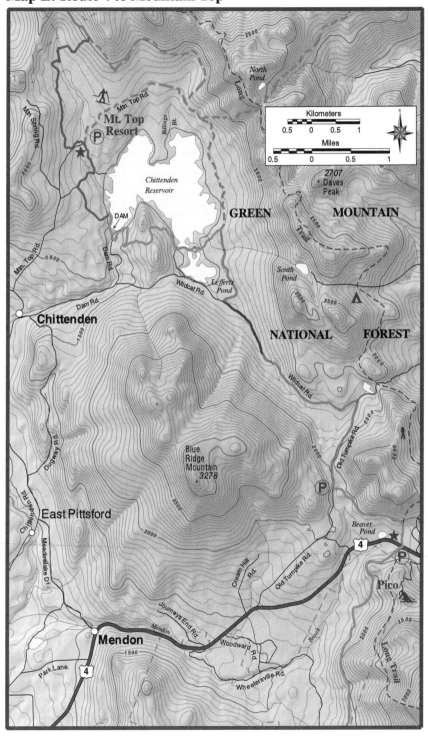

toward Route 4, or north to Mountain Top.

DISTANCE TO MAJOR LANDMARKS:

Start	Finish	Mileage	Total
Route 4 Parking Area	Old Turnpike Road	1.3	1.3
Old Turnpike Road	Log Landing	1.3	2.6
Log Landing	Wildcat Road plowing	1.5	4.1
Wildcat Road plowing	Logging road junction	1.0	5.1
Logging road junction	Round Robin junction	1.2	6.3
Round Robin junction	Chittenden Res. Dam	1.8	8.1
Chittenden Res. Dam	Mountain Top Ski Center	1.6	9.7

ROUTE DESCRIPTION:

From the Route 4 AT/LT/CT Parking Area, cross to the opposite side of Route 4 and head north into the woods on the AT/LT/CT. At 0.2 miles the Catamount Trail turns left (west) leaving the AT/LT. The CT heads west through the woods and soon joins a logging road, which it follows west to a "T" junction with another logging road, where it turns right (north) and heads steeply uphill. The CT reaches a height-of-land, descends sharply, then turns west and reaches a "T" junction with unplowed Old Turnpike Road (also VAST Corridor 7) at 1.3 miles.

Follow Old Turnpike Road north to a log landing at 2.6 miles, then turn left (west) onto Wildcat Road. Wildcat Road heads generally north, is unplowed for approximately 1.5 miles, then plowed for about 1.0 mile (it is often possible to ski here on snow-covered road or beside the road on snowmobile tracks). At a point 2.5 miles from the log landing (5.1 miles from Route 4) the Catamount Trail and VAST Corridor 7 leave Wildcat Road and head north on a logging road.

Follow the logging road north for 1.2 miles to a junction with the Round Robin (Mountain Top) XC ski trail. Turn left (west) here, leaving the VAST Trail, and follow Round Robin (generally broken but ungroomed) approximately 1.8 miles to a parking area just east of the dam at the south end of Chittenden Reservoir. Remove your skis and walk across the dam. (Alternate: follow the road south for several hundred yards to a "T" intersection with Dam Road. Turn right and head north to the west end of the dam.)

At the west end of the dam, follow the unplowed road north along the shore past several summer cottages and into the woods, where you will soon join Reservoir Run (Mountain Top) XC ski trail. Follow Reservoir Run north to a fork in the trail (take the right branch) and continue north to a "T" intersection with the Bounder Trail. Turn left (west) and follow Bounder to the plowed Mountain Top Road. Cross the road at Mountain Top Inn and head west, then north, across the open field to the Touring Center.

Touring Centers Along the Trail

All Catamount Trail Skiers using sections of the Trail that run through touring center trail systems are required to check in at the touring center and pay a trail fee. CTA members can get a half-price ticket upon presentation of their membership card (once at each center).

DAY SKI TOUR M:
MOUNTAIN TOP TO BLUEBERRY HILL

TOUR PROFILE:

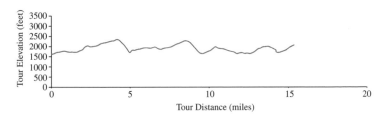

TOUR HIGHLIGHTS: A mostly groomed and rolling tour running along the VAST snowmobile trail and the groomed trails of Mt. Top and Blueberry Hill Ski Centers.

LODGING:
- See Lodging Tour L
- Blueberry Hill Inn, Goshen, 800-448-0707
- Churchill House Inn, Brandon, 802-247-3078
- Brandon Area Chamber of Commerce, 802-247-6401

STARTING POINT: Mt. Top Ski Center

FINISH POINT: Blueberry Hill Ski Center

TOTAL MILEAGE: 15.4

DIFFICULTY OF TOUR: Hard intermediate. Lots of climbing with some very steep descents.

ACCESS/EXIT POINTS:
1. Mt. Top Ski Center
2. River Road in Holden
3. Rte. 73 in Goshen
4. Blueberry Hill Ski Center

DIRECTIONS: **To Mt. Top:** Located on Mt. Top Rd. in Chittenden just off Chittenden Road (road to Chittenden Reservoir).

To Rte. 73: Connects Rte. 7 in Brandon and Route 100 in Rochester.

To Blueberry Hill: Located on Forest Service Rd.

Map M: Mountain Top to Blueberry Hill

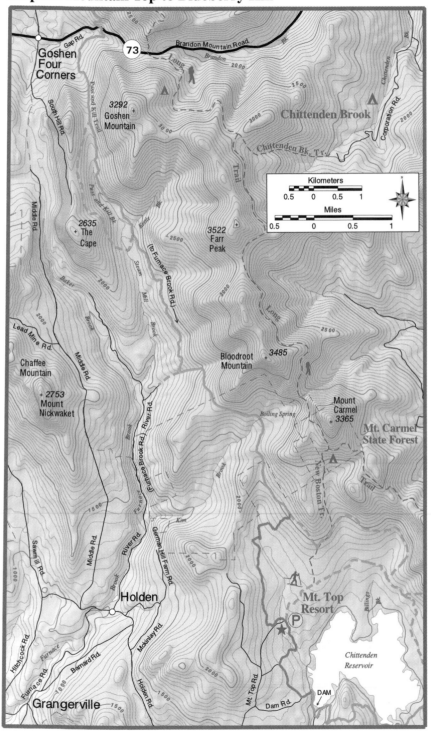

#32 (also called Goshen-Ripton Rd.) between
Routes 73 and 125.

DISTANCE TO MAJOR LANDMARKS:

Start	Finish	Mileage	Total
Mt. Top Ski Center	VAST Trail	1.0	1.0
(New Boston) VAST Trail	"Y" Junction	1.0	2.0
"Y" Junction	Furnace Brook	2.5	4.5
Furnace Brook	Puss and Kill	2.0	6.5
Puss and Kill	Rte. 73	3.5	10.0
Rte. 73	Power Line	0.5	10.5
Power Line	Road	1.75	12.25
Road	FSR 224	0.25	12.5
FSR 224	B.H. Ski Trails	1.0	13.5
B.H. Ski Trails	B.H. Ski Cntr.	1.9	15.4

ROUTE DESCRIPTION:

From Mt. Top X-C Center, proceed on Mt. Top's Hewitt Brook Trail to Deer
Run to Debonis Cutback (Intersection 48) to Lost Horizon (Intersection 47) to
an unnamed trail at Interection 56 to the New Boston Trail and VAST trail 7 at
Intersection 49, a "T" junction. Turn left on the VAST Trail, heading northwest
for 1 mile to a "Y" junction (1.0). At the junction, take the left fork, staying on
the main VAST trail. The left fork initially goes down a long and "do-able" hill,
after which it goes up a challenging steep hill and across a relatively flat stretch.
It then goes steeply down to the west. A sharp right turn toward the bottom of a
steep pitch puts you on gentler terrain for the 1/2 mile trek to Furnace Brook
Road (FSR #57). Note that while the Trail goes right on Furnace Brook Road, a
left turn will take the skier to River Road in Holden. Note also that within 1/4
mile of where you turn left, Furnace Brook Road is plowed.

Taking a right turn onto Furnace Brook Rd., the Trail heads north to a
clearing where the road ends (2.0). The Puss and Kill Trail goes north from the
clearing/end of road, climbing gradually to a notch on the shoulder of Goshen
Mountain and then descending a steep long hill towards Rte. 73.

The Puss and Kill will shortly descend a steep hill. Near the bottom of this
hill, watch for the Catamount Trail leaving to the right. Here the CT leaves the
Puss and Kill and VAST trails. It goes northeast in a gradual ascent on old roads
until a sharp left turn gets one across the Neshobe River on a new bridge. Rte.
73 is about 1/4 mile further (3.5).

Turn left onto Rte. 73 and go about 200 yds. down the hill to where an old
CVPS utility road goes rather sharply up hill to the Power Line (0.5). Turn left at
the Power Line and follow it northwest to a road (1.75). Turn right on the road
and walk to Forest Service Road #224 (0.25). FSR #224 leads through a Forest
Service blueberry management area to the trail system of Blueberry Hill XC
Center (1.0). Once on the Blueberry Hill system, follow the Hogback Trail to

trail numbers 25-27-15-11-7-3 to the XC Center and Inn (1.9).

There is a route to the Churchill House Inn. For more information on this route, contact the Churchill House at (802) 247-3078.

The 1988 End-to-End Relay gets ready to embark from Mt. Top Touring Center on the tour to Blueberry Hill.   *CTA file photo.*

DAY SKI TOUR N:
BLUEBERRY HILL TO NATURAL TURNPIKE

TOUR PROFILE:

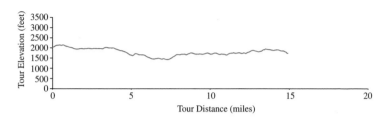

TOUR SNAPSHOT: Begins on the fine groomed trails of Blueberry Hill ski center, winds along an ungroomed backcountry segment to the Breadloaf campus and Rikert Ski Touring trail system and then on to the Natural Turnpike snowmobile trail.

LODGING:
- See Lodging Tour M
- Chipman Inn, Ripton, 800-890-2390
- Addison County Chamber of Commerce, 800-SEE-VERMONT

STARTING POINT: Blueberry Hill Ski Center

FINISH POINT: Natural Turnpike (Intersection of FSR 54 & 59)

TOTAL MILEAGE: 15.0 (9.5 miles to Rikert Ski Center)

DIFFICULTY OF TOUR: Intermediate. Rolling terrain, easy access, no major climbing or steep down hills.

ACCESS/EXIT POINTS:
1. Blueberry Hill Ski Center
2. Widow's Clearing Parking Area
3. Rte. 125
4. Rikert XC Center
5. Natural Turnpike (FSR 54/59 Intersection)

DIRECTIONS: **To Blueberry Hill Ski Center:** Located on Forest Service Road (FSR) 32, also called the Goshen-Ripton Rd, between Routes 73 and 125.

To Rikert Ski Center: Located on Route 125 in Ripton, Vermont.

Map N: Blueberry Hill to Natural Turnpike

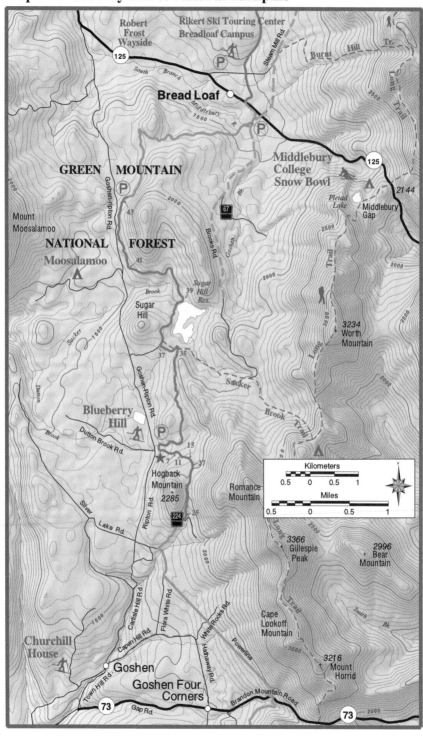

To Natural Turnpike: Follow plowed section of Natural Turnpike from Route 125 in Ripton.

DISTANCE TO MAJOR LANDMARKS:

Start	Finish	Mileage	Total
B.H. Ski Cntr.	Widow's Clearing Trail	6.0	6.0
Widow's Clearing Trail	FSR 67	3.0	9.0
FSR 67	Rte. 125 (Rikert X-C)	0.5	9.5
Rikert Ski Cntr.	Steam Mill Road	1.3	10.8
Steam Mill Road	FSR 59	1.2	12.0
FSR 59	FSR 54 Intersection	3.0	15.0

ROUTE DESCRIPTION:

From Blueberry Hill Ski Center head out behind the Inn on the Stewart Trail until it merges with the Sucker Brook Trail. Follow the Sucker Brook Trail to the Horseshoe Trail north to the edge of the Blueberry Hill trail system (ski trails 5-9-17-19-33-35-37-39-41-43 on Blueberry Hill X-C Map) (6.0). (Note: If you intersect FSR 32 from the Horseshoe Trail, you have missed a turn to the north, a few hundred yards back up the trail.)

From the edge of the trail system continue north a short way (0.2) to the Widow's Clearing Trail. (Forest Service parking area nearby on Goshen-Ripton Rd.) The Widow's Clearing Trail runs northeast, ending with a long downhill onto FSR 67 (3.0). Turn left on FSR 67 (also called Brooks Rd). Cross over the Middlebury River to a large field. The field leads to Rte. 125. Cross Rte. 125 to Thomas Trail on the Rikert X-C Center system and follow this trail to the Ski Center (0.5).

From Rikert X-C Center, follow the Myhre Trail across the plowed road and up the hill. At the fork, go right on the Frost Trail. The Trail continues to climb and then levels off. Take the next right onto the Holland Trail. Follow the Trail through the woods and around a Beaver Pond. As the Trail hooks back around to the west (left) and intersects the Frost Trail, turn right (east) on the Forest Service trail called Steam Mill Road (1.3). At this point the Catamount Trail leaves the Rikert Trail System. Follow Steam Mill Road east until it ends at the intersection with FSR 59 (a wide road, packed by snowmobiles) (1.2). Turn left onto FSR 59. Just after the open field and deer feeding area, follow the Cata-mount Trail to the right. The intersection of FSR 59 and 54 is one mile ahead and is a good place to position transportation. The road is plowed to this intersection.

CTA file photo.

Blueberry Hill Trail Map

There are many great ski trails in the Green Mt. National Forest between Rte. 73 and Rte. 125. Blueberry Hill Ski Center has an excellent map of these trails and can give you advice on where to go. To get a copy of their map, stop at their touring center on the Goshen - Ripton Rd., visit their website at www.blueberry hill.com, or call 800-448-0707.

DAY SKI TOUR O:
NATURAL TURNPIKE TO LINCOLN GAP

TOUR PROFILE:

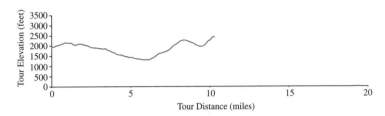

TOUR SNAPSHOT: Runs along snowmobile trails, a 1.5 mile backcountry trail, and ungroomed forest roads to the top of Lincoln gap where there are wonderful views. Involves a 2.6 mile road walk which can sometimes be skied.

LODGING: • See Lodging Tour N

STARTING POINT: Natural Turnpike (intersection of Forest Service Roads 54 & 59)

FINISH POINT: Lincoln Gap (closest access is in Lincoln on west side of the gap)

TOTAL MILEAGE: 10.35

DIFFICULTY OF TOUR: Easy intermediate until South Lincoln then mostly uphill.

ACCESS/EXIT POINTS: 1. Natural Turnpike FSR 54 & 59 intersection
2. South Lincoln Rd.
3. French Settlement Rd.
4. Lincoln Gap Rd.

DIRECTIONS: **To Natural Turnpike:** Follow plowed section of FSR 59 / Natural Turnpike from Route 125 in Ripton.

To Lincoln Gap: Take Lincoln Road from Route 116 in Bristol.

Map O: Natural Turnpike to Lincoln Gap

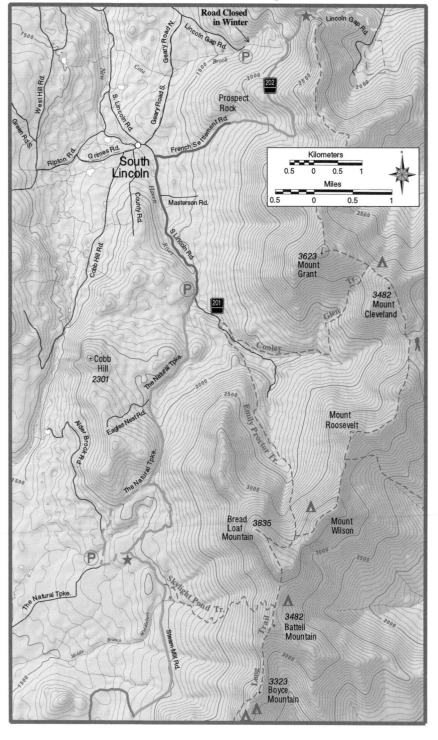

DISTANCE TO MAJOR LANDMARKS:

Start	Finish	Mileage	Total
FSR 54/59	Trail Head	0.7	0.7
Trail Head	FSR 59	1.5	2.2
FSR 54	Plowed Road	2.5	4.7
Plowed Road	French Settlement Rd.	1.5	6.2
French Settlement Rd.	End of Plowed Rd.	1.1	7.3
End of Plowed Rd.	FSR 202	0.75	8.05
FSR 202	Lincoln Gap Rd.	1.5	9.55
Lincoln Gap Rd	Top of Lincoln Gap	0.8	10.35

ROUTE DESCRIPTION:

The Trail actually begins on FSR 59 just east of the parking area at the junction of FSR 54 & 59. Follow FSR 59 (also a VAST snowmobile trail) east for about 0.7 miles to get to the Catamount Trail.

Turn left off the snowmobile trail following the CT blazes into the woods. The Trail soon enters a clearing then runs back into the woods along a stream. Bear left over a bridge and uphill. The Trail follows a route that gradually levels off coming to a "T" intersection.

Turn right here and follow the Natural Turnpike (FSR 54) north. At this point FSR 59 is plowed for one mile, ski on the shoulder. Resume skiing on the full width of the road. This section ends with a long downhill. Plowing begins at the bottom of the hill (2.5).

Currently, you have to walk or ski along the plowed shoulder of the South Lincoln Rd. towards South Lincoln. Just before South Lincoln take the second right onto French Settlement Rd. Proceed 1.1 mi. up the road to the end of plowing. You can ski from here straight ahead uphill on a wood road. Soon you will pass a cabin on the left, please stay on the Trail. It is PRIVATE PROPERTY. After passing the cabin you are entering U.S. Forest Service land. Follow the Trail ahead passing over a stream and into a recently logged area. The Catamount Trail goes into the woods again and shortly meets with a gate at FSR 202 (8.05). Ski north on FSR 202 to its junction with Lincoln Gap Rd. To continue on the Catamount Trail north, or to get to Warren, turn right and ascend the gap. To get to the end of plowing in South Lincoln, turn left and descend.

Join the Catamount Trail Association!

At the Catamount Trail Association, members are everything. Since its inception in 1984, members have been the driving force behind this incredible Vermont treasure. The members of our association are volunteers, financial contributors and make up the rich character of our organization. We couldn't accomplish much of what we do without the loyalty and strong commitment of our members. Nearly 60% of the money it takes to protect and manage the Trail comes from our membership. Won't you consider joining this special group who give their time and resources to make sure back-country skiing in Vermont is available to everyone? Check out our website: www.catamounttrail.together.com for more information, volunteer opportunities and specific tours. Better yet, ski a few miles of the 300 that await you.

Membership benefits include:
- Half price skiing for one day at more than 20 of Vermont's best cross-country ski
  centers, a member benefit valued at $150
- The Catamount Trail News (3 issues) and Winter Events Calendar
- Free participation in tours and events
- Discounts at selected retailers and on CTA merchandise
- **Peace of mind that comes with knowing the Catamount Trail will be there for generations to come because**
YOU took action

DAY SKI TOUR P:
LINCOLN GAP TO MAD RIVER BARN

TOUR PROFILE:

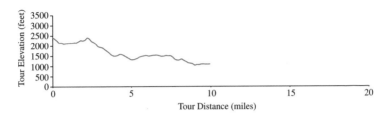

TOUR SNAPSHOT: Fun descent from Lincoln Gap, rolling terrain of Sugarbush Golf course and winding wooded traverse through the Mad River Valley and Sugarbush Resort.

LODGING:
- Sugarbush Inn, Warren, 800-53-SUGAR
- Hamilton House, Warren, 800-760-1066
- West Hill House, Warren, 802-496-7162
- Mad River Barn, Fayston, 800-631-0466
- Tucker Hill Lodge, Fayston, 800-543-7841

STARTING POINT: Lincoln Gap

FINISH POINT: Mad River Barn

TOTAL MILEAGE: 10.0

DIFFICULTY OF TOUR: Advanced/Intermediate to Sugarbush Inn. Easy/Intermediate from the Inn to Mad River Barn (requires snowplow and herringbone).

ACCESS/EXIT POINTS:
1. Lincoln Gap Rd.
2. West Hill Rd.
3. German Flats Rd.
4. Rte. 17
5. Mad River Barn

DIRECTIONS: **To Lincoln Gap:** Access from the west is closed to vehicles during the winter due to the road not being plowed. You can park your car however, at the plow turn around on the west of Lincoln Gap and

Map P: Lincoln Gap to Mad River Barn

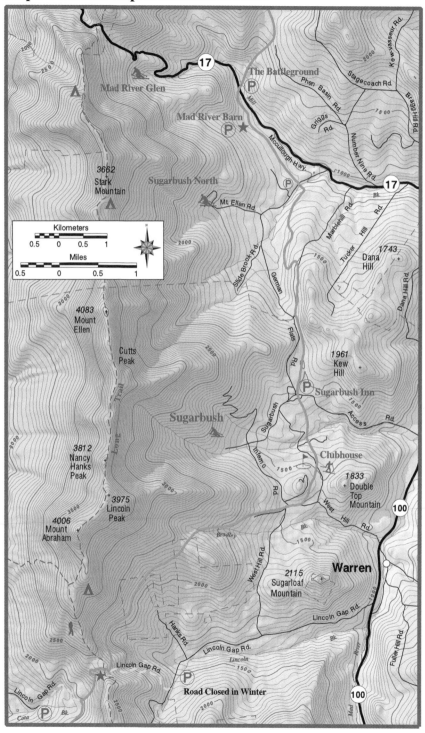

ski over the gap which is a short but very steep climb. From the east you can access Lincoln Gap from Warren.

To Sugarbush Inn: On Sugarbush Access Rd. off Route 100 in Warren.

To Mad River Barn: On Route 17 in Fayston.

DISTANCE TO MAJOR LANDMARKS:

Start	Finish	Mileage	Total
Top of Lincoln Gap	Plowed Rd.	1.0	1.0
Plowed Rd.	Start of Sugarbush Inn Trails	3.25	4.25
Inferno Rd.	Sugarbush Inn	2.25	6.5
Sugarbush Inn	German Flats Rd.	2.5	9.0
German Flats Rd.	Mad River Barn	1.0	10.0

ROUTE DESCRIPTION:

NOTE: Currently, the Catamount Trail route is waiting landowner and Forest Service approval from Lincoln Gap to West Hill Road. This route has not been blazed and is not yet an established trail nor part of the Catamount Trail system. We hope it will be open by Winter 2001. Please call the CTA office for an update on the status.

Until the new route is finalized, skiers can ski from the top of Lincoln Gap down the east side on the unplowed road to where it meets West Hill Rd. (2.25). Skiers can then ski along the edge of the road until they get to the intersection of West Hill Rd. and the Inferno Rd. (2.0).

At the intersection of West Hill Rd. and Inferno Rd., cross onto the golf course and ski north towards the lower golf course. You will pass the golf course clubhouse. Ski downhill along woods to cross Norwegian Rd., down a steep hill, across a bridge and up the other side on ski center trails toward the Sugarbush Inn. (2.25).

Before reaching the Sugarbush Inn, the Catamount Trail passes beside Pavilion Recreation Center tennis courts and crosses the Access Road just downhill or east of the Inn. The Trail passes below Sugarbush Inn parking lot and next to a beaver pond where it enters the woods. It ascends a plateau. After the plateau, it shortly descends a steep hill leading to a series of beaver ponds. The Trail follows the chain of ponds, paralleling the German Flats Rd. which will be seen on the left. A short ways after the Beaver ponds, the Trail will pass by some new home sites, by the Sugar Run Condos, and then onto a old class IV road, which eventually becomes the Marble Hill Rd. Watch for a left turn off the road which will take you downhill on a long "S" curve. The Trail continues gradually down and across the hill until it turns left to drop down to a bridge before crossing German Flats Rd. just south (0.1 mile) of Fayston Elementary School (a good place to park on the weekends). (2.5)

Cross the road and pick up the Trail on the other side. The Trail enters a mature evergreen woods and gently rolls along past a few houses and more woods. After a final stretch through some sharp dips, the Trail enters a meadow below Mad River Barn. (1.0)

DAY SKI TOUR Q:
MAD RIVER BARN TO CAMELS HUMP SKIERS ASSOC.

TOUR PROFILE:

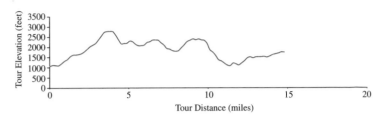

TOUR SNAPSHOT: A challenging mostly backcountry tour takes one up over Huntington Gap and then through the wilds of Camels Hump State Park to the trail system of the Camel's Hump Skiers Association. Wonderful views.

LODGING: See Lodging Tour P

STARTING POINT: Mad River Barn

FINISH POINT: Camels Hump Skiers Association Trails

TOTAL MILEAGE: 14.85

DIFFICULTY OF TOUR: Advanced and very remote.

ACCESS/EXIT POINTS:
1. Mad River Barn
2. Carse Rd. in Hanksville (Beane Trail)
3. Trapp Rd.
4. Camels Hump Rd. (Forest City)
5. Camels Hump Skiers Association

DIRECTIONS: **To Mad River Barn:** On Route 17 in Fayston, four miles west of intersection of Routes 17 and 100.

To Camels Hump Skiers Association: Take East Street to Bert White Rd. in Huntington.

DISTANCE TO MAJOR LANDMARKS:

Start	Finish	Mileage	Total
Mad River Barn	Phenn Basin	1.5	1.5

Map Q: Mad River Barn to Camels Hump Skiers Association

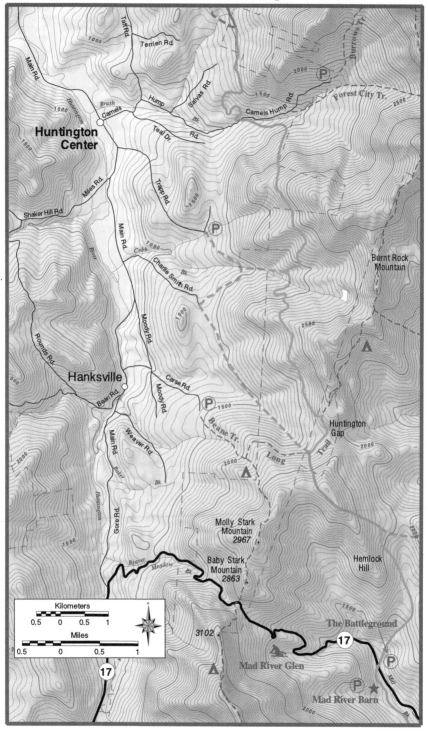

Phenn Basin	VAST Trail	1.2	2.7
VAST Trail	Huntington Gap	1.8	4.5
Huntington Gap	Cobb Brook	2.7	7.2
Cobb Brook	Camels Hump Rd.	3.1	10.3
Camels Hump Rd.	Pasture/Wood's Edge	0.75	11.05
Pasture	South Edge of Nordic Trails	1.8	12.85
South Edge of Nordic Trails	CHS Association	2.0	14.85

ROUTE DESCRIPTION:

From the Mad River Barn head north east onto the open meadow along the west side of Rte. 17. Cross Rte. 17 by the bridge for the Battleground condominiums. Stay to the west of the brook and head northeast through the field at the entrance to the Battleground, paralleling Rte. 17. Go by the tennis courts, along the side of the condo woodshed, and then turn east over a bridge on a logging road. Follow the logging road to a junction in a clearing. The CT turns right following a logging road uphill by a brook. The Trail then climbs steadily until it reaches a beaver pond and large open meadow called Phenn Basin.

From Phenn Basin, turn left and follow a logging road (which is sometimes groomed for snowmobiles) uphill gradually. The Trail crosses a brook and continues to climb more steeply until it intersects with a VAST Corridor snowmobile trail. Turn left and follow the VAST trail as it heads north and ascends the steep ridge of Hemlock Hill. The ridge affords great views of the Mad River Valley. (Be wary of snowmobile traffic in this area.) The Trail continues north following the ridge line and then descends sharply down the west side of the ridge. Leveling out, it meets the Long Trail (white paint blazes) at Huntington Gap.

At this intersection, the VAST trail descends to the west and provides a possible access/exit point at the Beane Trail and Carse Rd. (Follow the VAST trail one mile west to an intersection with a logging road on the left (west) which leads to the Beane Trail and Carse Rd. 0.75 miles.)

To continue on the Catamount Trail at Huntington Gap, leave the VAST trail and follow the Long Trail north approximately 200 feet before veering off the Long Trail to the left. After 1.5 miles, the Catamount hits an old logging road for a fun, winding, northwesterly descent. At the bottom, the Trail crosses a bridge over Cobb Brook and emerges into a clearing. The access trail which enters the clearing from the left rejoins the VAST trail (0.5 miles), which runs north to the end of Trapp Road (0.75), another good exit point. From the clearing, the CT enters the woods to the right and follows an old logging road. The Trail now climbs steadily to 2400 feet, where it levels off a bit affording a rest and great views. Continuing north, the Trail eventually meets a steep access road where it turns left (west) and descends. The road is extremely steep in places and at one point offers a tremendous view of Camels' Hump. At the foot of the hill, the road intersects another road. Turn left and ski out to Camel's Hump Rd.

Turn right onto Camels Hump Road and look for a river crossing immediately to your left (near the culvert). Blazes will take you across the river and up onto the bank on the other side. (Although the river is shallow here, use extreme caution when crossing). The Trail parallels the river and eventually climbs up onto a shelf where it takes a sharp right turn up an old access road to the farm fields (0.25).

The Trail circumnavigates the perimeter of the farm fields, climbing up into the highest meadows where you will see spectacular views of the Huntington Valley. Look for the blazes on the fence posts or nearby trees. The Trail eventually enters the woods to the right (0.5) and climbs gradually through a series of switchbacks, eventually passing an abandoned sugar house.

From here, the Trail follows a gently winding, northerly course to the southeast corner of Camels Hump Skiers Association trails at the Dead River Run/Skunk Brook trail intersection (1.8). The most direct route to the Skiers Association access is to follow Skunk Brook to Toothacker Swamp to Gullywumper to Pond Road.

Camels Hump Skiers Association

The Camels Hump Skiers Association is a non-profit group of local skiers who have banded together to maintain the beautiful ski trails of the former Camels Hump Nordic Ski Center in Huntington. To help them maintain the trails and parking lot, the group requests that users buy a day or season membership. Skiers seeking access to the Catamount Trail may also use the parking lot, provided they pay a fee. For more information call 802-434-4760.

DAY SKI TOUR R:
CAMELS HUMP SKIERS ASSOCIATION TO BOLTON VALLEY SKI TOURING CENTER (VIA HONEY HOLLOW TRAIL)

TOUR PROFILE:

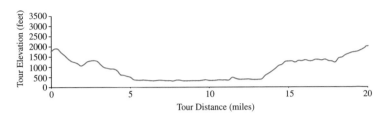

TOUR HIGHLIGHTS: Starting on the Camels Hump Skiers Association trail system, this tour runs through ungroomed terrain mostly downhill to Jonesville. After a 7 mile road walk to get around the Winooski River, the trail heads uphill to Bolton Valley Ski Area on a VAST snowmobile trail and Bolton Valley Cross-Country trails.

LODGING:
- Bolton Valley Inn & Resort, Bolton, 802-434-3444
- Black Bear Inn, Bolton, 800-395-6335
- Winter Camping at Bryant Lodge (contact Bolton XC Center at 802-434-3444)

STARTING POINT: Camels Hump Skiers Association

FINISH POINT: Bolton Valley Ski Touring Center
(Popular alternatives are to ski just the Honey Hollow Trail to Jonesville or from Bolton down to Rte 2.)

TOTAL MILEAGE: 20.7 miles- including 7.5 mile drive (Honey Hollow Trail is 6.9 miles, Bolton to Rte 2 is 6.3 miles).

DIFFICULTY OF TOUR: Short but with steep downhills and narrow chutes.

ACCESS/EXIT POINTS: 1. Camels Hump Skiers Association
2. Jonesville Rd.- Honey Hollow Parking Area

Map R: Camels Hump Nordic Ski Center to Bolton Valley

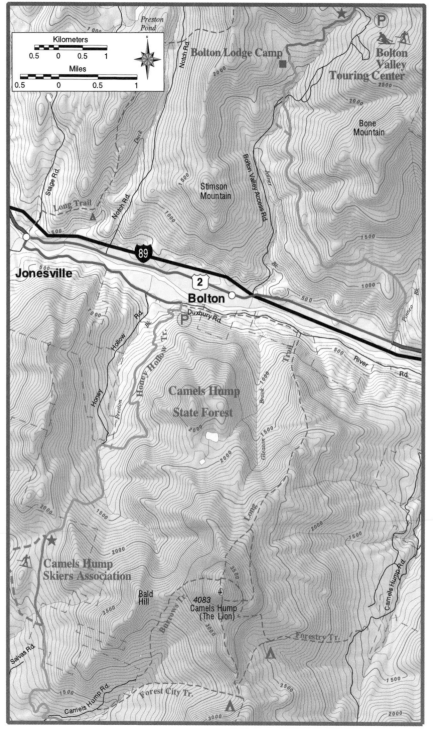

3. Rte. 2, 1.9 m. east of Bolton Valley Access Rd.
4. Bolton Valley Ski Touring Center

DIRECTIONS: **To Camels Hump Skiers Association:** Follow East Street to Bert White Rd. from Huntington.

To Honey Hollow Parking Area: Located on River Road, 2.2 miles east of the metal bridge in Jonesville.

To Bolton Valley Ski Touring Center: Located at the Bolton Valley Ski Resort. Follow Bolton Valley Access Road from Route 2 in Bolton.

DISTANCE TO MAJOR LANDMARKS:

Start	Finish	Mileage	Total
Camels Hump Center	Honey Hollow Trail	1.8	1.8
Honey Hollow Trail	Ridge Line	0.1	1.9
Ridge Line	Woods Rd.	1.5	3.4
Woods Rd.	Gate	0.8	4.2
Gate	Steep Gully	0.7	4.9
Steep Gully	Logging Road	1.6	6.5
Logging Road	Parking Lot (end H. H. trail)	0.4	6.9
Parking Lot	Rte. 2-Trail Jct.	7.5	14.4
Trail Jct.	VAST #2	0.7	15.1
VAST #2	Bolton Valley Access Rd.	3.5	18.6
Access Road	Broadway	0.5	19.1
Broadway	Bolton Valley Ski Center	1.6	20.7

ROUTE DESCRIPTION:

From the Camels Hump Skiers Association Parking Lot, take the access trail from the road through the field to head out on Pond Road to Woodchuck Ramble and Logger's Loop east to the Honey Hollow trail head (1.8). The Honey Hollow Trail climbs to a ridge line overlooking Honey Hollow and the shoulder of Camels Hump (the mountain) (0.1). From the ridge line (entering State Land), you will descend through a series of chutes and traverses, ending on a wood road (1.5). Turn north (left) and go downhill on the road. At the bottom of a fairly steep schuss, bear right and uphill through a gate (0.8). Pass through the gate and ski a road until the blue blazes enter into the woods again on the left (0.2). The Trail will merge into a logging road (1.6), which leads down to the Honey Hollow parking area provided by the Vermont Department of Forests, Parks and Recreation (0.4).

The route to Bolton Valley XC Center resumes on the north bank of the Winooski River approximately 3.0 miles east of where the Honey Hollow trail ends on the south bank. Do not attempt to cross the river! (We hope to have a bridge some day). Drive west on the River Rd. to the Jonesville Bridge (2.2). Take Route 2 east past the Bolton Valley access road. (3.4) Continue past a large trailer park and a driving range until you reach a dirt road on the north side of Rte. 2 (1.9) The road is just west of where Rte. 2 crosses Pinneo Brook, and quickly narrows into a secondary snowmobile trail which serves as the Catamount Trail as well. Avoid parking on the private property at the head of the trail.

The ski trail follows the secondary snowmobile trail and climbs alongside Pinneo Brook to a major intersection with a primary VAST #2 snowmobile trail (0.7). Follow VAST #2 west, then turn right to leave the snowmobile trail just before it crosses the Bolton Valley Access Road (3.0). The ski trail heads north and crosses the access road higher up (0.5). Across the road, the ski trail climbs northwest. You will pass by a gravel pit and a leach field, staying to the right. The Trail emerges onto the trail network of Bolton Valley Ski Touring Center at Broadway, near the old Bolton Lodge. (0.5) Follow the groomed trail, Broadway, up the hill to the Touring Center (1.6).

Northern VT Adventure Ski Map

The Northern VT Adventure Ski Map, available through the Catamount Trail Association office (802-864-5794) and many other retail stores, shows most of the trails in the Mt. Mansfield area, including the interconnected, four-touring center, trail network of Stowe. It is a great map to have if you plan on doing any skiing in Bolton, Stowe or Underhill.

DAY SKI TOUR S:
BOLTON VALLEY SKI CENTER TO TRAPP FAMILY LODGE

TOUR PROFILE:

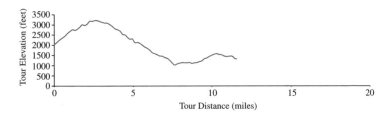

Tour Distance (miles)

TOUR HIGHLIGHTS:	Rugged back-country tour climbing 1000 feet and descending 2000 feet featuring marvelous views of the Winooski Valley, ridgeline skiing, and a long descent through open forest. Good early/late snow.

TOUR HIGHLIGHTS: Rugged back-country tour climbing 1000 feet and descending 2000 feet featuring marvelous views of the Winooski Valley, ridgeline skiing, and a long descent through open forest. Good early/late snow.

LODGING:
• See Lodging for Tour R
• Trapp Family Lodge, Stowe, 800-826-7000
• Stowe Area Association, 800-24-STOWE

STARTING POINT: Bolton Valley Ski Center

FINISH POINT: Trapp Family Lodge

TOTAL MILEAGE: 11.75

DIFFICULTY OF TOUR: Advanced: very long, steep and isolated.

ACCESS/EXIT POINTS:
1. Bolton Valley Ski Center
2. Nebraska Valley Rd.
3. Trapp Family Lodge

DIRECTIONS:
To Bolton Valley Ski Center: Located off Route 2 in the town of Bolton.

To Trapp Family Lodge: Located off Luce Hill Road in Stowe.

To Nebraska Valley Rd. Parking: About 3 miles south of Stowe, turn west onto the Moscow/ Nebraska Valley Rd. and go 5 miles to a roadside

Map S: Bolton Valley Ski Center to Trapp Family Lodge

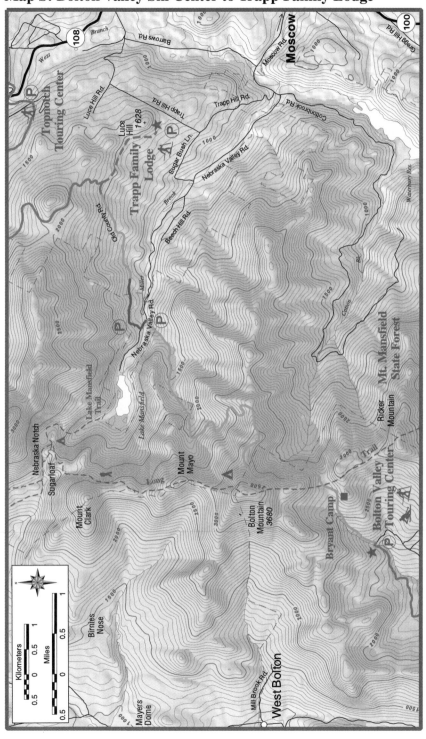

parking area. If this area is full, go 100 yards further to the Old County Rd. There is a large parking area 0.1 mile up this road.

DISTANCE TO MAJOR LANDMARKS:

Start	Finish	Mileage	Total
B.V. X-C Cntr.	Bryant Lodge	1.0	1.0
Bryant Lodge	Cotton Brook/Trapp Trail	0.5	1.5
Cotton Brook/Trapp Trail	3300'	0.75	2.25
3300'	Shoulder-Bolton Mt.	0.75	3.0
Shoulder-Bolton Mt.	Stream at 2300'	2.50	15.5
Stream	Sugar House	1.25	6.75
Sugar House	Nebraska Valley Rd.	1.5	8.25
Nebraska Valley Rd.	End of Plowing on O.C. Rd.	0.75	9.0
End of Plowing	Russell Knoll	1.0	10.0
Russell Knoll	Trapp Family Lodge	1.75	11.75

ROUTE DESCRIPTION:

The Trail begins at the Bolton Valley XC Center (2000'), and goes uphill to Bryant Lodge (2700'). The most direct route is Bryant Trail, and thence to the lodge (1.0). (The most scenic route to the lodge is via Gardner's Lane and then turning left onto North Slope, coming out at a trail intersection just above Bryant Lodge.) From the lodge, the route continues uphill past the intersection with the North Slope Trail, where it turns north (left). The route now traverses relatively flat terrain on a marked Bolton Valley trail (Birch Loop), rising gently to 2800'. Upon reaching a trail fork, Birch Loop turns left and the Catamount Trail goes to the right heading north. After about 100 feet the Cotton Brook Trail turns off to the right, the Catamount Trail continues straight ahead. (0.5) From here the Cotton Brook trail drops off the side of Bolton Mt. following Cotton Brook and emerges on the Cotton Brook Rd. after about six or seven miles.

The Catamount Trail rises steeply uphill and enters a series of switch-backs. After straightening out, it heads basically north/northwest, coming to an intersection with the Raven's Wind Trail of Bolton Valley at about 3300'. (Raven's Wind is for experts only.) Raven's Wind goes left as the Catamount Trail heads up and right. The Catamount then stays at a fairly constant elevation, with first gentle and then abrupt ups and downs. It skirts the east shoulder of Bolton Mt. (entering State Land), then goes through a series of steep ups and downs, and can be difficult to follow (0.75). East of the summit of Bolton Mt., the route turns sharply east (right) following the ridge running east from the mountain. (It is easy to miss this turn if not paying attention.) The route then winds along the ridge, with many tight turns and short, quick ups and downs. There are a couple of good viewpoints overlooking Cotton Brook Basin and south to Camels Hump. This is a good spot for a lunch break. Most of the difficult climbing is now behind you.

Near the end of the ridge, the Trail begins dropping north and northwest in a series of long switch-backs. Caution is needed at the end of one of the switch-backs, as a new trail, locally known as the J-K Trail, heads right and toward Cotton Brook while the Catamount Trail swings sharply left in a switch-back. The Trail continues through switchbacks and over some small stream crossings. After a short rise, the route traverses downward, ending abruptly in a steep stream crossing, which often has open water. The elevation is now 2300' (2.5).

From the 2300' elevation line, the Trail drops steeply then switches back through open woods. It then returns to parallel the stream, drops steeply into a side stream crossing and bridge, then descends steadily to near a sugar house (1.25). Just above the sugar house, during a moderate descent, there is a stream crossing bridged by a fairly narrow culvert- be careful! A long, gentle slope follows, then a steeper drop beside a stream gorge, eventually ending at the parking area on Nebraska Valley Rd. (0.75). This is a good bail out point for those desiring a shorter tour.

At the road, the Trail turns west for a road-walk of 100 yards. Turn northeast (right) onto the "Old County Road". This road is plowed to a house (0.7) then becomes a ski trail again. The Trail then follows the old trace of the county road to the maintained Trapp Family Lodge trails at Russell Knoll. (1.0) This portion of the road has eroded and captured a stream, making the Trail go from one side of the road to the other. From Russell Knoll follow the Trapp trail signs for the Russell Knoll Track, and then the Sugar Road to the XC center. (1.75)

The Slayton pasture cabin at the Trapp Family Lodge in Stowe.   *CTA file photo.*

DAY SKI TOUR T:
TRAPP FAMILY LODGE TO EDSON HILL

TOUR PROFILE:

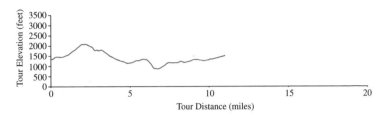

TOUR SNAPSHOT: This section runs almost entirely on the groomed trails of Stowe's four touring centers and includes a few hefty climbs and descents.

LODGING:
- Topnotch, Stowe, 800-451-8686
- Edson Hill Manor, Stowe, 800-621-0284
- Trapp Family Lodge, Stowe, 800-826-7000
- Mt. Mansfield Hostel, 802-253-4010
- Stowe Areas Association, 800-24-STOWE

STARTING POINT: Trapp Family Lodge

FINISH POINT: Edson Hill Touring Center

TOTAL MILEAGE: 11.5

DIFFICULTY OF TOUR: Advanced intermediate. 90% on groomed ski center trails with several options for shorter ski tours.

ACCESS/EXIT POINTS:
1. Trapp Family Lodge Touring Center
2. Stowe Mt. Resort Touring Center (Rte. 108)
3. Topnotch Touring Center (Rte. 108)
4. Wiessner Woods (on Edson Hill Rd.)
5. Edson Hill Touring Center

DIRECTIONS: **To Trapp Family Lodge:** From I-89 exit 10 in Waterbury, go north on Rte. 100 for 7.5 miles. Turn left onto Moscow Rd. Go 1 mi. and turn right onto Barrows Rd. Go to stop sign (Ten Acres Lodge on left). Turn left and follow signs to Lodge.

Map T: Trapp Family Lodge to Edson Hill

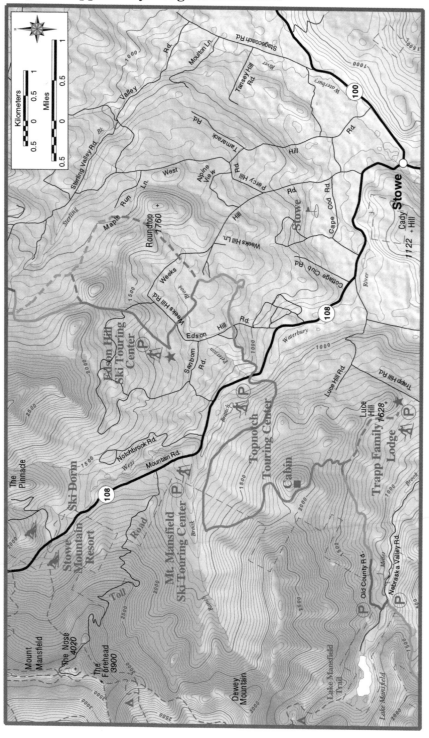

To Edson Hill Manor: From junction of routes 100 and 108 in Stowe village, take Rte. 108 north for about 4 miles. Turn right onto Edson Hill Rd. Go about 1 mile and take a left hand fork. Follow signs.

NOTE: On this tour you will ski through the trail systems of all four Stowe ski centers and therefore, you will need a trail pass. Purchase a pass wherever you park your car and start the tour.

DISTANCE TO MAJOR LANDMARKS:

Start	Finish	Mileage	Total
Trapp Family Ski Center	The Cabin	3.0	3.0
The Cabin	Ranch Camp Trail	0.7	3.7
Ranch Camp Trail	Ranch Valley Cruise	1.3	5.0
Ranch Valley Cruise	Lower Valley View	1.8	6.8
Lower Valley View	Topnotch Meadows	0.9	7.7
Topnotch Meadows	Topnotch Resort	0.5	8.2
Topnotch Resort	Edson Hill Rd.	1.0	9.2
Edson Hill Rd	Gameroff Sugarhouse	1.0	10.2
Gameroff Sugarhouse	Edson Hill Center.	1.3	11.5

ROUTE DESCRIPTION:

This section runs almost entirely on groomed trails of Stowe's four ski touring centers: Trapp Family Lodge, Stowe Mt. Resort Touring Center, Topnotch Resort and Edson Hill Manor. A one mile segment between Topnotch and Edson Hill Manor, including a stretch through the Wiessner Woods (owned by the Stowe Land Trust) will likely be well-travelled, yet ungroomed. Many possibilities exist for shorter tours covering one or two of the three legs are feasible, and the numerous touring center trails allow for many loop tours.

From the Trapp Family Lodge Touring Center, take Sugar Road or Russell Knoll Track to Picnic Knoll (about 1.2 m, mostly flat). From the Picnic Knoll, you can take either Parizo (uphill on your right) or Owl's Howl (straight ahead) to the Cabin Trail where you will turn left. After this steady climb of 1.8 m., you will reach Trapp's Slayton Pasture Cabin at the height of land. The cabin (open 10 a.m. - 3 p.m.) is a great place to buy snacks or lunch, dry out by the fireplace, and bundle-up for the breezy descent. From the cabin, continue west, then north (right) onto the Haul Road, which offers spectacular views of Mt. Mansfield and Smuggler's Notch.

The first groomed trail on your left, after about 0.6 m. of steady descent, will be Ranch Camp Trail, which connects the Trapp and Stowe Mt. Resort trail networks. Ranch Camp Trail traverses for a kilometer +/- before plunging into Ranch Camp Valley. After approx. 1.8 m., the Ranch Camp Trail ends at a

4-way junction.

If you plan to finish or make a pit-stop at the Stowe Mt. Resort Touring Center, take a right onto the Burt Trail, then left on Crosscut 1 or 2, then right onto Timberlane - about 2 to 3 m. total, mostly downhill.

If you want to bypass the Stowe Mt. Resort Touring Center, backtrack from the 4-way intersection about 100 feet, and turn right to ski Ranch Valley Cruise to its end at the Stowe Derby Trail (1.5 to 2 m. in all). Turn right onto the Stowe Derby Trail (you are now on the Topnotch trail network). The Derby Trail intersects the Adams Camp Trail after about 0.6 m. Continue straight, traversing, passing just above a townhouse complex, and meeting the Lower Valley View Trail at a cleared knoll. Turn left, plunging down the "Pipeline" Trail and out into a farm meadow on the valley floor. Here, turn left onto Meadow Trail. After 300-500 meters, join the Stowe Recreation Path and cross a pedestrian bridge. Topnotch TC is about a one mile, easy ski upstream along the West Branch of the Little River.

From Topnotch's TC, cross to the north side of Rte. 108. After only 50 meters, cross a footbridge, and turn left. The Trail ascends a ravine for 200 - 300 meters, between the brook and Topnotch Townhouses. At the back of the townhouse development, the Trail turns sharply to the right, and continues 100 meters or so, then left on Deer Run. Climbing for approx 300 meters, Deer Run merges (more like a sharp right turn) with Rivendale Trail. You are now leaving Topnotch's trail network. After 200 meters, look for an unnamed path on your left leading into the pastures of the Peterson Brook Farm. A knoll offers a panoramic view of Stowe. Hug the fence for 200-300 meters and follow the blazes until the driveway of Peterson Brook Farm intersects Edson Hill Road (paved). Cross the road and ski under the power line into Wiessner Woods, owned by the Stowe Land Trust. The parking lot here is a convenient intermediate starting/finishing point.

Ski by the parking area and find a commemorative marker/ trail head. Take note that blue diamonds, similar to CTA's, have been used to mark walking trail loops in Wiessner Woods. Follow the CT paw prints through Wiessner Woods for approx 0.6 m, and join the Heading Home Trail at a renovated sugar house. Follow CT blazes on the Heading Home Trail gradually up and out to a field, then left along the perimeter of the field to a sign post. Follow the West Hill Trail (maintained by Edson Hill TC) through swampy woods, crossing a driveway and a subdivision road, then another 0.5 m.(+/-) until you meet a dirt, town road. Cross the road and follow CT blazes to Edson Hill Ski Touring Center (approx 500 meters).

DAY SKI TOUR U:
EDSON HILL TO FARM RESORT

TOUR PROFILE:

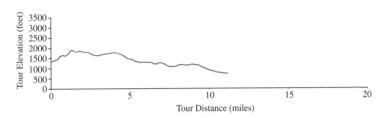

TOUR SNAPSHOT: This tour travels groomed ski center trails, ungroomed backcountry terrain, snowmobile trails, open farm fields and a golf course, gently losing elevation along the way. A side trail connects to Beaver Meadow and Burling Camp.

LODGING:
- See Lodging Tour T
- Farm Resort, Morrisville, 800-822-4353

STARTING POINT: Edson Hill Ski Center

FINISH POINT: Farm Resort (Rte. 100)

TOTAL MILEAGE: 11.0

DIFFICULTY OF TOUR: Intermediate

ACCESS/EXIT POINTS:
1. Edson Hill Ski Center
2. Sterling Brook Rd.
3. Mud City Loop Rd.
4. Cole Hill Rd.
5. Farm Resort (Rte. 100)

DIRECTIONS: **To Edson Hill Ski Center:** Located on Edson Hill Road off Route 108.

To Farm Resort: Located on Route 100 in Morrisville, 5 miles north of Stowe.

To Sterling Falls Gorge: Take the Stagecoach Rd. off Rte. 100 (north of Stowe) to Sterling Falls Rd.

Map U: Edson Hill to Farm Resort

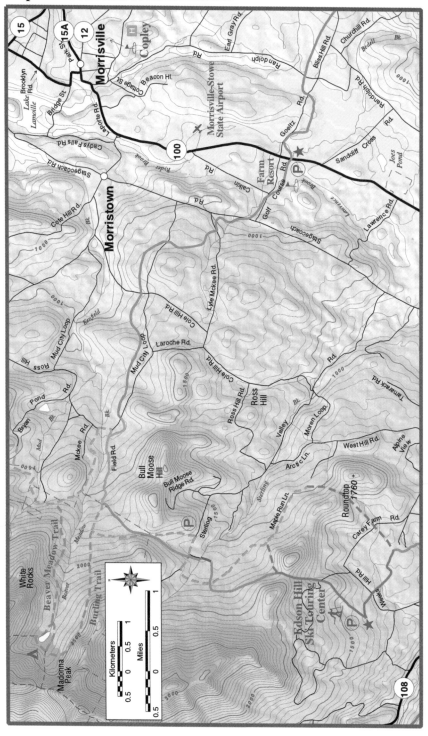

Follow Sterling Falls Rd. to Sterling Forest Town Parking Area.

DISTANCE TO MAJOR LANDMARKS:

Start	Finish	Mileage	Total
Edson Hill Touring Cntr.	Ridge at edge of E.H. Trail System	1.3	1.3
Ridge	Marston Trail	1.3	2.6
Marston Trail	Maple Run Lane	0.4	3.0
Maple Run Lane	Sterling Brook Rd.	0.3	3.3
Sterling Brook Rd.	Corn/hay Field	1.6	4.9
Corn/hay Field	Cole Hill Rd.	3.1	8.0
Cole Hill Rd.	Lyle Mckee Rd.	1.5	9.5
Lyle Mckee Rd.	Farm Resort	1.5	11.0

ROUTE DESCRIPTION:

From the Edson Hill XC Center, the Catamount Trail follows the Edson Hill trail Penn Station to Billings Road to the top of a ridge (intersection with Adam's Climb). Go left here towards Sterling Valley on an old road (1.5).

Soon after you begin descending, the Catamount Trail turns left off the road and into the woods of the Sterling Forest. The Trail glides through the forest, coming to a "T" with another trail (called the Marston Trail) after 1.3 miles. Turn right, descending and cross a VAST snowmobile trail. At the bottom of the hill, turn left at the "T" junction with "Maple Run Lane" and ski out to the plowed road and Sterling Falls Gorge. Turn left and walk or ski across the bridge. There is a small place to park here.

Put your skis back on and climb the snowbank. Continue north skiing along the fence line. The Trail turns at the fence corner and follows it west a bit, where it turns into the woods, heading north again. About 100 yards after, you will cross a plowed drive that goes to a large parking lot. Continue on, cross the snowmobile trail, heading north through the forest. You will be on an old logging road. This climbs very gradually for 0.5 miles or so, then reaches a flatter, wetter area at the top of the pass and begins gradually descending. Next, you'll come out to a wide State access road and snowmobile trail. Take a right to go downhill. You'll head downhill gradually, cross a couple of small streams, and then come out in a corn/hay field (2.5).

Continue in a roughly eastern direction across the field, heading downhill and following the snowmobile trail. Follow the snowmobile trail at the east edge of the field- it goes through the tree line and behind a yellow house. It will then cross the Mud City Loop Rd. and continue through fields on the north side of the road. At the top of the field, the Trail follows a powerline, then bends left into the woods before entering the top of another field. The Trail leaves the snowmobile route here and makes its way through numerous fields that parallel the Mud City Loop Road.

There will be a few fence crossings, a short piece in a power line cut, and when you get close to the farm, there may be some cows in a small area of the field. Stay to the north side of the house and barns watching for CT markers at fence line and stonewall crossings. At the end of the field, the Mud City Loop Rd. "T"s into Cole Hill Rd. and there is a house on the corner. (1.75) The route crosses the road and continues traveling east on another old town road, which is also a snowmobile trail. It climbs up fairly steeply from the plowed road, then levels off, then goes downhill. Next you'll come to an old building in a clearing on your right. The Trail turns south (right) here, proceeds across the clearing, and goes back into the woods. Follow the blazes as the Trail follows some logging roads before coming out on a paved road (Lyle McKee Rd). (1.5)

Follow the Lyle McKee Road 100 yards to the left, then take a right just past the first drive and out into the fields to the east of the house with a silo attached. Ski down the field toward a farm and Stagecoach Rd. You must cross Stagecoach Rd. near the bottom of the field, and follow a cow path until it crosses a stream at the bottom of the hill to the field on the other side. Ski diagonally across this field to the southeast corner where you can cross a dirt road onto the golf course of the Farm Resort. Continue downhill parallel to the road until you come to the Farm Resort and Route 100. (1.5)

Volunteer for the Trail

The Catamount Trail was built and is maintained each year by member volunteers. Each fall, groups of members walk each section of Trail, clearing brush and ensuring that the route is well marked. With 300 miles of Trail, it's a big job and we always need lots of help.

You can help by joining one of our fall trail work days. They are a great opportunity to meet other CTA skiers, to get outside in the crisp autumn air, to enjoy the colors of the autumn leaves, and to do some valuable volunteer work. To find out about the work days, contact us at our office, look in the Catamount Trail Newsletter, or visit our website at www.catamounttrail.together.com.

DAY SKI TOUR V:
FARM RESORT TO ROUTE 15

TOUR PROFILE:

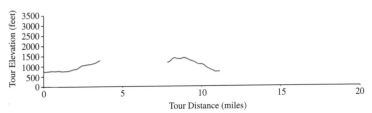

TOUR SNAPSHOT: Primarily a back-country tour climbing gently out of the Rte. 100 valley offering great views of Mt. Mansfield while skiing through open fields.

LODGING: • Farm Resort, Morrisville, 800-822-4353
• Golden Maple Inn, Wolcott, 800-639-5234

STARTING POINT: Farm Resort (call ahead for permission if you wish to park at the Farm Resort: 800-822-4353)

FINISH POINT: Rte. 15 (Leriche Farm)

TOTAL MILEAGE: Farm Resort to Lahey Rd.: 3.7
Elmore to Rte. 15: 3.5

DIFFICULTY OF TOUR: Intermediate.

ACCESS/EXIT POINTS: 1. Farm Resort
2. Randolph Rd.
3. Lahey Rd. (near Bliss Farm)
4. Village of Elmore, Elmore Store
5. Rte. 15 by the Leriche Farm

DIRECTIONS: **To Farm Resort:** 6.5 miles north of Stowe on Route 100.

To Elmore Village & Store: On Route 12 by Lake Elmore, approximately 5 miles east of Morrisville.

Map V: Farm Resort to Route 15

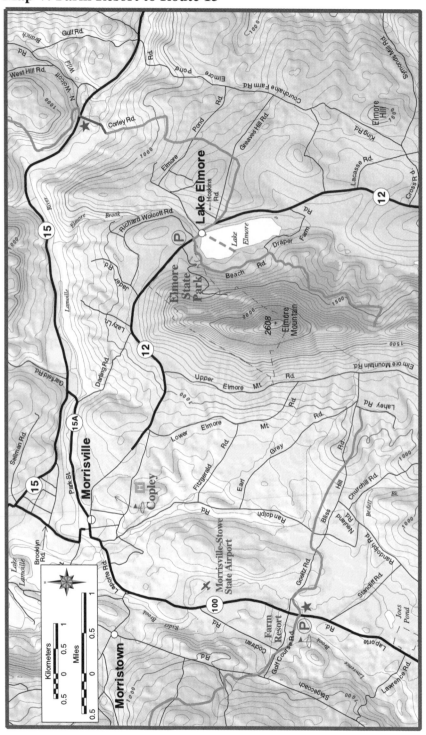

To Rte. 15 by the Leriche Farm: The Leriche Farm is at the intersection of the North Wolcott Rd. and Rte. 15 between Wolcott and Morrisville. There is a dirt road opposite the farm and North Wolcott Rd. Park along this dirt road.

DISTANCE TO MAJOR LANDMARKS:

Start	Finish	Mileage	Total
Farm Resort	Randolph Rd.	1.2	1.2
Randolph Rd.	Bliss Hill Rd.	1.5	2.7
Bliss Hill Rd.	Lahey Rd.	1.0	3.7
Missing Trail			
Elmore Store	Rte. 15	3.5	3.5

ROUTE DESCRIPTION:

NOTE: *Due to a closure by a landowner, we currently have a gap in this section between Lahey Rd. and the top of the Elmore Mt. Work is currently underway to re-connect this route.*

Farm Resort to Lahey Rd:

From the Farm Resort, cross Rte. 100 and ski diagonally across a field (about 200 yards) northeast to Goeltz Rd. Ski or walk east along Goeltz Rd. You'll cross a bridge and in a few hundred yards (where the trees end and where there's a large animal pen usually with llamas) you'll see CT blazes on your right heading into a large field. Follow the blazes and blue flagging around the perimeter of the field and through a short wooded section into an area of dead trees (a swamp in the summer). At the end of the swamp, you'll cross Goeltz Rd. and continue into a large field marked by CT blazes on stakes. Cross Randolph Rd. and continue up through a smaller field to a treeline. Here the CT enters the woods and winds through some lovely evergreens. The next couple of miles are easy skiing along wide logging roads and through open fields, and may even be groomed by a landowner.

The next road crossed is Bliss Hill Rd., and soon after that you'll ski through a large, flat field, eventually passing within 50 yards of a small house (Bliss Farm). Here you re-enter the woods for a short section before reaching Lahey Rd. This is where the Trail currently ends due to landowner request. Ahead of you is another large field with a farmhouse and distinctive silo at the far end of it. Elmore Mountain goes right up behind the farm.

Elmore to Rte. 15:

From the Elmore Store, cross Rte. 12 and ski south on VAST snowmobile trail #15 for 0.2 mi. to Greaves Hill Rd. Leaving the snowmobile trail, cross Greaves Hill Rd. and look for an opening in the hedgerow with a Catamount blaze set back from the road (to discourage snowmobile use). The Trail heads into a clearing and toward a red barn. Passing by the barn, ski uphill through a meadow marked with blazes on stakes. Enter the woods and soon you'll be in a small sugarbush. Please be careful of the maple sap lines which cross the Trail several times. Continue through an area of thick, high brush on either side of the Trail. When you get to a snowmobile trail, go straight across it and uphill into some softwoods. Catamount blazes continue for another half mile before the Catamount Trail intersects VAST snowmobile trail #100 A at a "T" junction where you will take a left turn. The Catamount blazes end here. Continue on #100 A (which has a nice variety of wooded trails, open northerly views, and is mostly downhill) for 1.6 miles. When you get to the bottom of a long, straight downhill run on an unplowed road, leave VAST 100A which makes a right turn. To reach Rte. 15, continue straight ahead on the plowed road for 0.7 miles.

Skiing through the fields along Bliss Hill Road on the Farm Resort to Rte. 15 section.
Photo by Rosemary Shea.

DAY SKI TOUR W:
RTE. 15 TO CRAFTSBURY NORDIC CENTER

TOUR PROFILE:

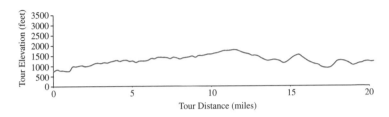

TOUR SNAPSHOT:	Ski on snowmobile trails, ungroomed terrain and finally, the groomed trails of the Craftsbury Nordic Center.
LODGING:	• Golden Maple Inn, Wolcott, 800-639-2534 • Craftsbury Outdoor Center, Craftsbury Common, 800-729-7751 • Craftsbury B&B, Craftsbury Common, 802-586-2206 • Inn on the Common, Craftsbury Common, 800-521-2233
STARTING POINT:	Leriche Farm at Rte. 15
FINISH POINT:	Craftsbury Nordic Ski Center
TOTAL MILEAGE:	21.35
DIFFICULTY OF TOUR:	Advanced intermediate: Very long but with good access and exit points.
ACCESS/EXIT POINTS:	1. Leriche Farm at Rte. 15 2. Garfield Rd. (about five miles north of Rte. 15) 3. Eden Rd. 4. Rte. 14 5. Craftsbury Common 6. Craftsbury Nordic Ski Center
DIRECTIONS:	**To Leriche Farm:** Located at intersection of Route 15 and North Wolcott Road, 5.7 miles east of intersection of Routes 15 and 100.

Map W Part 1: Route 15 to Wiley Brook

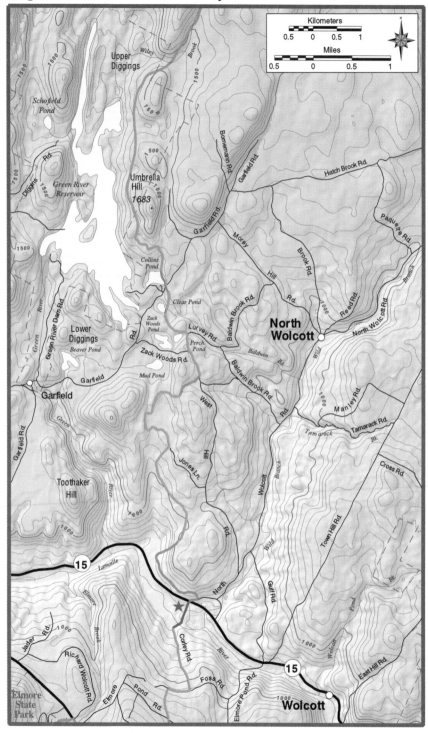

Map W Part 2: Wiley Brook to Craftsbury Nordic Center

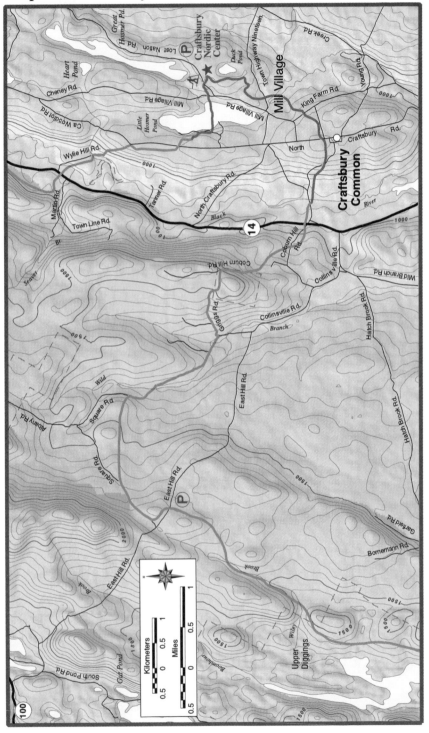

To Crafsbury Nordic Ski Center: Located on dirt road off the main Craftsbury Rd. just north of Craftsbury Common. Or, just follow the signs from Rte. 14.

DISTANCE TO MAJOR LANDMARKS:

Start	Finish	Mileage	Total
Leriche Farm	Power Line	0.75	0.75
Power Line	Poker Ride Snowmobile Tr.	0.6	1.35
Snowmobile Trail	Plowed Rd.	1.2	2.55
Plowed Rd.	Small Stream	0.2	2.75
Small Stream	Log Landing	0.8	3.55
Log Landing	Large Field	0.8	4.35
Large Field	Garfield Rd.	1.6	5.95
Garfield Rd.	1st VAST Fork	1.7	7.65
1st VAST Fork	2nd VAST Fork	2.2	9.85
2nd VAST Fork	Eden Rd.	2.4	12.25
Eden Rd.	Town Road	2.0	14.25
Town Road	Brown House	1.3	15.55
Brown House	Green House	0.5	16.05
Green House	Red House	1.3	17.35
Red House	Rte. 14	0.7	18.05
Rte. 14	Unplowed Rd.	0.4	18.45
Unplowed Rd.	Craftsbury Common	0.7	19.15
Craftsbury Common	Beige House	0.2	19.35
Beige House	Hosmer Pond Drainage	0.5	19.85
Drainage	Dirt Rd.	0.2	20.05
Dirt Rd.	Duck Pond Trail	0.5	20.55
Duck Pond Trail	Craftsbury Nordic Center	0.8	21.35

ROUTE DESCRIPTION:

The Trail begins with a short, steep climb up a farm road on the Leriche Farm. The road is located just east of a barn on the north side of the North Wolcott Rd. The road leads to an open pasture and a power line running east to west (0.75). The Catamount Trail runs northwest and parallel to the power line, descending into a steep ravine, passing over a narrow bridge and up a short hill. At this point, a green shed is visible on Rte. 15 on the left and the power line closes in on the right. The Trail continues to the right up the ravine to an old wooden fence.

Passing through the wooden fence, the Trail climbs northward through woods, crosses a dirt road and after 0.6 miles turns left onto the VAST Poker Ride snowmobile trail. This trail curves northwest then north through woods for about 1.2 miles, emerging for about 0.2 miles on a plowed but probably unsanded road (Jones Lane). The Trail then takes a sharp left (north) turn onto an unimproved logging road (a few yards after passing a small stream which crosses the road in a culvert) that leads to a log landing (0.8). The Trail takes off to the west (left) side of the log landing on a combination of old logging road and narrow ungraded segments in a northwest direction to a large field. (0.8) The Trail proceeds diagonally left across the field to an unplowed road. Follow the unplowed road to a snowmobile trail that bears right (north) and comes to a "T" with another snowmobile trail which runs north/south. Turn left (west) and wind through a series of ponds to Garfield Road (1.4). Turn right crossing Garfield Road to Collins Pond Road (0.1). This road may be plowed in certain sections and may be used for logging; please use caution. Follow this road until you reach a fork in the VAST trail (1.7). Bear right.

After the fork, the Catamount Trail crosses Wiley Brook (2.0). The VAST trail again forks in 0.2 miles. Bear right (north) and travel north on the west side of Wiley Brook (0.7). Recross Wiley Brook and continue north on the east side of the brook. Pass a large beaver pond on the right, climb to a log landing and follow logging road to Eden Road (1.7).

Cross the Eden Road and follow a snowmobile trail north, then east descending 400 feet to an unplowed town road (2.0). Go right (south).

From the intersection, follow the Trail to a brown house and a plowed dirt road. (1.3) Continue on the dirt road southeast to a green house. (0.5) The Trail then bears left on a driveway and then turns right onto a lightly used snowmobile trail and climbs 400' to a saddle. (0.7) From the saddle, turn southeast (right) and descend to the unplowed Colburn Hill Rd. through fields and hedgerows until you see a red house. (0.6) Before reaching the house, cross through a field and descend through pasture land on an old town road to a gateway by Rte. 14. (0.7)

Cross Rte. 14, pass a large red barn and follow a plowed dirt road as it crosses the Black River. Take the dirt road until it intersects an unplowed town road on the right. (0.4) Turn right onto this road as it climbs sharply to a paved road on the north end of Craftsbury Common. (0.7) Cross the paved road, north of the Common, to the Center Common trail. Follow the Center Common trail across fields to a road to the north of a beige house. (0.2) Cross the road and descend to the drainage from Hosmer Pond. (0.5) Climb through fields to a dirt road (0.2) Cross the road and continue to the Duck Pond trail. (0.5) Go left on the Duck Pond trail to the Craftsbury Nordic Ski Center. (0.8)

Become a Trail Chief

A Trail Chief is a member-volunteer who is responsible for maintaining one of the twenty-six sections of Catamount Trail. Trail Chiefs monitor their section of Trail annually, lead fall trail work days to clean the annual brush off the Trail, contact landowners, find alternate routes when needed, and sometimes lead tours.

To be a Trail Chief, all you need is an interest in helping and a little spare time to spend outside on the Trail- we can help you with the rest. It's a great opportunity to meet like-minded people, spend time outdoors, learn about trail management and give back to a resource you love. If you are interested in becoming a Trail Chief, please contact the Catamount Trail Association office to learn more about it. Become part of the team!

DAY SKI TOUR X:
CRAFTSBURY NORDIC SKI CENTER TO LOWELL GENERAL STORE

TOUR PROFILE:

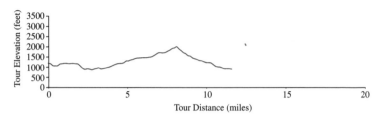

TOUR SNAPSHOT: A part snowmobile trail (60%), part back-country (25%), part groomed cross-country ski trail (15%), this tour crosses the Lowell mountains and travels through many open farm fields.

LODGING:
• See Lodging Tour W
• Village House Inn, Albany, 802-755-6722

STARTING POINT: Craftsbury Nordic Ski Center

FINISH POINT: Lowell General Store

TOTAL MILEAGE: 11.9

DIFFICULTY OF TOUR: Long, intermediate tour.

ACCESS/EXIT POINTS:
1. Craftsbury Nordic Ski Center
2. Nelson Rd. in Albany
3. Rte. 100 in Lowell

DIRECTIONS: **To Craftsbury Nordic Ski Center:** Located on a dirt road just north of Craftsbury Common.

To Lowell General Store: Located in the village of Lowell 0.25 miles south of the intersection of Routes 100 and 58 (Note that Route 58 west of town is not plowed in winter). To get to the Catamount Trail, go 100 feet south of the store on the opposite side of the road (east side). Go up a steep hill between two houses (about 50 feet back from the road).

Map X: Craftsbury Nordic Center to Lowell General Store

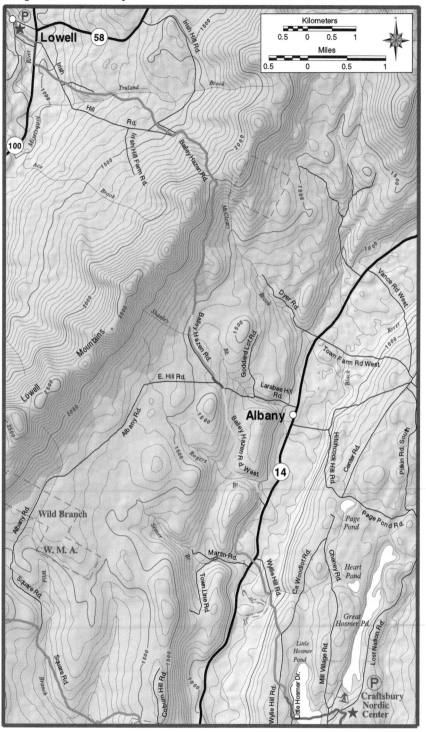

DISTANCE TO MAJOR LANDMARKS:

Start	Finish	Mileage	Total
Craftsbury Center	West shore of Little Hosmer	0.9	0.9
Little Hosmer Lake	VAST #14N	0.7	1.6
VAST #14N	Rte. 14	1.5	3.1
Rte. 14	Bayley Hazen Rd.	0.6	3.7
Bayley Hazen Rd.	Nelson Farm, VAST #58	2.7	6.4
VAST #58	Peon Farm	3.5	9.9
Peon Farm	Lowell General Store	2.0	11.9

ROUTE DESCRIPTION:

From the Craftsbury Nordic Ski Center head to Little Hosmer Pond by Trail #7. Cross the lake, skiing west towards a red house on the west shore of the lake (0.9). Climb the bank north (right) of the house and follow the trail north to a large field (0.5). At this point you leave the groomed trails. Go right in the field and proceed until you intersect the snowmobile trail VAST #14N where it enters a plowed road (0.2). Continue north on the other side of the road until it intersects an unplowed road (0.6). Take the road down the hill (plowing resumes at the bottom), cross the bridge over the Black River and then cross Rte. 14 (0.9). Enter the field on the south side of a large barn. Circle behind the barn and continue north through fields paralleling Rte. 14 to a driveway leading up to a log house and sawmill (0.6). Join the old Bayley-Hazen Military Road here and begin the ascent of the Lowell range. This is the trail you will follow into Lowell.

The Trail crosses Rodgers Brook and then continues up through a hemlock-lined ravine to a large pasture (0.9). Follow an old roadway, lined with stone walls and maple trees, from the west side of the pasture to the driveway of a dairy farm (0.8). Take the driveway and bear left on a plowed road (0.1). Follow the road to another intersection and bear right. (0.1) Continue beside this plowed road to the Nelson's Farm called "Breezy Acres" (0.8). This point is marked by a Bayley Hazen historic sign. At the farm, the plowing ends and the road continues as a snowmobile trail (VAST #58). The Trail climbs 650' to open fields and crests at 2120' (2.5). The Trail then descends 600' to a paved road at the Peon Farm (1.0). Cross the road and continue descending into the valley via the fields of Peon Farm. As you enter the woods, you will cross two small bridges. The snowmobile trail continues from here crossing a paved road (1.4). It then crosses some flat fields and enters the woods for a short steep plunge to Rte. 100 and the Lowell General Store. (0.6)

VISIT OUR WEBSITE

at
www.catamounttrail.together.com
to find:

•The latest Guidebook Updates

•Upcoming events

•Ski conditions

•CTA products and ordering

•Membership & Association Info

•Post a report of your last ski trip on the Trail

•Read trip reports posted by others

DAY SKI TOUR Y:
L0WELL GENERAL STORE TO JAY PASS (HAZEN'S NOTCH NORDIC CENTER)

TOUR PROFILE:

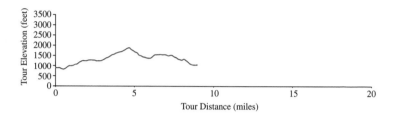

TOUR SNAPSHOT: A part back-country, part snowmobile trail following the historic Bayley-Hazen Military Rd. over Hazen's Notch.

LODGING:
- Hazen's Notch B&B, Montgomery Ctr., 802-326-4708
- Black Lantern Inn, Montgomery, 800-255-8661

STARTING POINT: Lowell General Store

FINISH POINT: Jay Pass (Rte. 242)

TOTAL MILEAGE: 8.9 (Lowell to Hazen's Notch Nordic Center)

DIFFICULTY OF TOUR: Intermediate

ACCESS/EXIT POINTS:
1. Rte. 100 - Lowell General Store
2. Rte. 58 Jct. with Mine Rd.
3. Rte. 58 - Western Terminus of Plowed Rd.
4. Hazen's Notch Nordic Center

DISTANCE TO MAJOR LANDMARKS:

Start	Finish	Mileage	Total
Rte. 100 - Lowell	Bayley-Hazen Rd. sign	0.1	0.1
Bayley-Hazen Rd. sign	Rte. 58	0.2	0.3
Rte. 58	Power Line	0.7	1.0
Power Line	Barn-Start of BH Rd.	0.7	1.7
Barn	VAST #58	0.5	2.2
VAST #58	Rte. 58	1.4	3.6

Map Y: Lowell General Store to Hazen's Notch Nordic Center

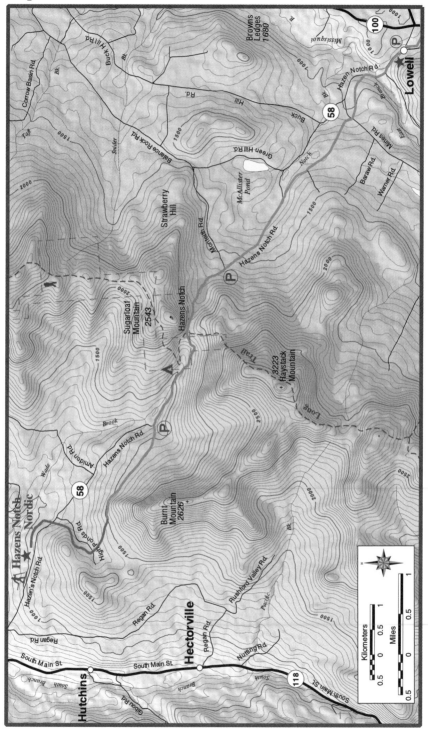

| Rte. 58 | Begin Plowed Rte. 58 | 2.8 | 6.4 |
| Plowed Rte. 58 | Hazen's Notch Nordic | 2.5 | 8.9 |

ROUTE DESCRIPTION:

NOTE: Currently this route ends at Hazen's Notch Ski Center. The route is incomplete from Hazen's Notch Ski Center to Jay Pass.

The Catamount Trail crosses Rte. 100 in Lowell (0.1). The Trail bypasses the center of Lowell coming out by a church on the south side of Rte. 58. (0.2) Here you will have to take off your skis and walk through a built-up area crossing two branches of the Missisquoi River. After the second bridge look for a large power line crossing the road. (0.7) After a short clamber up the bank to the west of Rte. 58, put your skis back on and follow the power line west. You will go through a gateway in a large stone wall emerging into an open pasture. Continue west towards a large barn and house on opposites sides of the road. Cross to the north of the buildings. (0.7)

At this point you will be on the Bayley Hazen Military Road. Along this section, which is a lovely old tree-lined lane, climb steadily to an intersection with VAST #58 entering from the south. (0.5) The Catamount Trail continues northwest with VAST #58 on the Bayley Hazen road until it rejoins Rte. 58. (1.4) From the point where the trail rejoins Rte. 58, the road climbs steadily 500' to the height of land at 1800' and then descends steeply 500' to a point 100 yards before the end of the snow covered road. (2.8) Here, **before** the beginning of the plowed road, the Catamount Trail makes an abrupt left turn and ascends around and over a short rise uphill from the road. The Trail then levels off and begins a long gradual descent of 500' on the Hazen's Notch trail, Beaver Pond Trail and East Meadow Trail to Hazen's Notch Cross-country Ski Area. (2.5)

The Catamount Trail is currently incomplete from the Hazen's Notch Ski Center to Jay Pass. We are currently looking for volunteers to help us with this re-establishment of the route. If you would like to help, please contact the CTA office at (802) 864-5794.

Skiing through Hazen's Notch. *CTA file photo.*

DAY SKI TOUR Z:
JAY PASS TO CANADIAN BORDER

TOUR PROFILE:

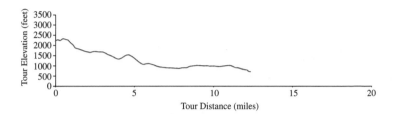

TOUR SNAPSHOT: A mostly back-country tour involving a total drop of 1,000 feet from Jay Pass to Jay village and then flat terrain from Jay village north. The Trail currently does not reach the US/Canada border. This section is north facing and gets massive snow accumulation (great early/late snow).

LODGINGS:
- See Lodging Tour Y
- Jay Peak Area Association, 800-882-7460
- Jay Peak Resort, Jay, 802-988-2611
- Jay Village Inn, Jay, 802-988-2306
- Cedar Wood Lodge, Jay, 802-988-4459
- Inglenook Lodge, Jay, 800-331-4346

STARTING POINT: Jay Pass (Rte. 242)

FINISH POINT: Border of Canada & Vermont

TOTAL MILEAGE: 12.5

DIFFICULTY OF TOUR: Intermediate and strenuous due to very deep snow (often 3 feet) with a very steep hill in the first mile (this can be avoided with a bypass route).

ACCESS/EXIT POINTS:
1. Jay Pass (Rte. 242)
2. Inglenook Lodge
3. Shallowbrook Rd.
4. Lucier Farm Rd.
5. Jay Village (Rte. 242 & Cross Rd.)
6. Mayhew Rd.

Map Z: Jay Pass to Canadian Border

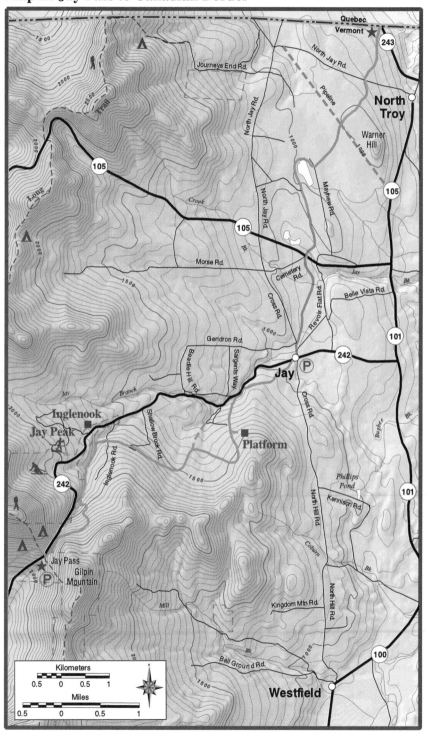

DISTANCE TO MAJOR LANDMARKS:

Start	Finish	Mileage	Total
Jay Pass	Stream at the bottom	1.0	1.0
Stream at the bottom	Exit for Inglenook	1.0	2.0
Exit for Inglenook	Shallow Brook Rd.	0.5	2.5
Shallow Brook Rd.	Lucier Farm Rd.	1.5	4.0
Lucier Farm Rd.	Road going to the platform	1.5	5.5
Road going to the platform	Jay Village	1.0	6.5
Jay Village	Canadian Border	6.0	12.5

ROUTE DESCRIPTION:

NOTE: This section begins at 2000 feet, climbs gradually for half a mile, then drops 500 feet in the second half mile. In icy or crusty conditions or for those seeking a gentler ski, use the bypass route to avoid this first mile (see BYPASS ROUTE, below). In addition, the last 2 miles to the US/Canada border cannot be skied due to a logging project (see last paragraph of route description).

From Jay Pass, the Trail begins on an old logging road at the east end of the parking lot on the south side of the highway. Look carefully because the snowplow can easily hide the trail entrance. The Trail ascends moderately before leveling off 500 feet above Rte. 242. The Catamount Trail turns left at the first fork in the road. It then starts to descend and makes a sharp left turn followed by a sharp right turn, and begins to drop again, gradually turning left and becoming steeper as it begins the final drop to the stream at the bottom. DIFFICULT CROSSING- BRING A METAL SCRAPER BECAUSE YOUR SKIS MAY GET WET. We will build a bridge over the stream eventually.

There is a bypass route which is not very well marked, although some markers are present. This route can be used if you want to avoid the first mile with its steep downhill.

BYPASS ROUTE: Coming from Jay Village, just before you get to the top of 242, there is a parking lot on your left. Follow the contours of the land across the stream to join the Catamount, approximately 250 ft. into the woods from the road. Not very well marked, although some markers are present.

After the difficult stream crossing, the Trail continues along the stream for about one mile, where it crosses the stream again (another DIFFICULT CROSS-ING). Here you bear right and the Trail will start downhill before reaching an open meadow. This road has been used extensively by skidders in the last few years. Stay on your left along the edge of the trail or you may fall in the big wet holes in the road. To stay on the Catamount Trail, keep to your right and you will be heading towards the Shallowbrook development. If you cross left over the stream here (used to be a bridge), you will reach the Inglenook Lodge and Rte. 242 in approximately 500 feet.

The Trail now ascends for the next half mile where there has been logging in our favor: TELEMARKER'S PARADISE. There is a trail that runs from the top of the ridge on your right side, all the way down to the stream on your left side. You can easily spend a few hours playing in here. (Anyone interested in telemarking only could access this section via the Inglenook entry point and spend the day in this beautiful area.)

To continue on the Catamount Trail, follow the logging road to a dead end. At the dead end, make a sharp turn to your right, going uphill (better be waxed properly because it's fairly steep for 100 feet or so). The Trail will bring you to the Shallowbrook Road (a narrow bridge crosses over the ditch). Directly ahead, you re-enter the woods and come to the pumphouse for the Shallowbrook development.

CAUTION: The next mile or so gets overgrown quickly and sometimes looks not very well maintained. It is very well marked, however, so if you take your time to identify the next marker as you go, you will be okay.

When you reach the pumphouse, head towards your right and you will reach a very obvious old road going downhill. Keep following the markers all the way down to the Lucier's farm meadow (about a mile or so), crossing two difficult large gullies along the way. Views of Owl's Head, Elephant and Orford mountains, all in Canada, greet you when you reach the meadow. If you cross the field directly ahead, you reach the Lucier Farm Road which leads to another exit point on Rte. 242. (A car can be left there, late in the season, when there is not enough snow to ski at lower elevations.)

To continue on the Catamount Trail, keep to the right side of the field and cross the brook over a small bridge to re-enter the woods. Climb an old logging road to the top of a small meadow and again re-enter the woods by crossing a small bridge. Immediately after this bridge, you make a sharp right turn. The Trail climbs for a while through a beautiful pine and cedar forest. Pay careful attention here, because there are several 90 degree turns over the next half mile or so. You will eventually reach another road which was built for a real estate project that tried to link the Town of Jay to the Town of Westfield (on the other side of the ridge), but was abandoned about 25 years ago. The Catamount Trail goes down that road and makes a 90 degree turn to the right. Continuing on for about 400 feet or so, you will cross another small logging road. The Catamount Trail goes straight through the woods towards Jay Village. If you want to stop at a nice spot for lunch, make a sharp right, and go uphill on that road. There you will find a hunting platform, with a table, chairs, etc. which the landowner allows us to use, providing we respect the privilege and leave no trace of our use. The platform is on the left and can be easy to miss (five minutes of climbing maximum).

Continuing straight on the Catamount Trail (instead of stopping for lunch) will lead you through a beautiful pine forest to a small field. Keep following the markers on your left to find an old logging road going through a maple forest. The logging road will lead you to a "T" intersection. The Catamount Trail turns left, going down to another meadow. Keep to your right to re-enter the woods on a trail that used to be part of the Cedar Wood Lodge trail system about 25 years ago. At the end of this trail, you will reach a big pile of dirt. Keep to your left along the snowmobile trail going toward Jay Village. Once you reach the Cedar Wood Lodge, keep going past the front yard, down towards the Jay Country Store. Across the street from the Jay Village Store is the Jay Village Inn which is a wonderful place to stop for a good meal or an overnight, before you continue on (the lasagna is excellent).

From the Jay Country Store, walk east on Rte. 242 to its junction with the Cross Road. Turn left and walk across the bridge over Jay Branch Brook. Start skiing here following the main snowmobile trail east. You will go over a snowmobile bridge to enter a cedar forest (be careful on the curve because the snowmobilers can't see you that well here). You will soon reach the intersection of Cemetery Road and Rte. 105. Cross Rte. 105 directly in front of you and follow the snowmobile trail for the next 100 feet or so. At the top of the hill, the Catamount Trail leaves the snowmobile trail on the left. When you reach the next field, go directly ahead along its edge, bordering the forest that edges the properties on your right (you actually go through backyards). You will reach a smaller, private snowmobile trail which has very little snowmobile traffic. Keep following the Catamount markers until you reach a field that will bring you to the edge of a large beaver pond, (it actually looks like a small lake). Follow the markers around the pond. (DO NOT CROSS THE POND IN THE MIDDLE.) You then exit the pond area on the right side through a series of well-marked roads, and reach a small cabin where you can stop for a break.

Re-enter the woods, following the markers, to reach another small beaver pond. Stay to your right, and keep looking for markers on your right through this messy area. Just after leaving this beaver pond you will join a road going slightly uphill for the next mile. You will eventually reach the pipeline area, which is essentially a large snowmobile highway in the winter.

Currently, YOU MUST STOP HERE AND CAN NOT GO ANY FUR-THER ON THE CATAMOUNT. The hill in front of you on your right is called Warner Hill and was logged during the summer of 1998. The logging obliterated the Trail and we are working on identifying a route to reconnect with the US/Canada border in North Troy. Keep an eye on the Catamount Trail web site (www.catamounttrail.together.com); it's possible we will have found an alternate route for the 1999-2000 season.

NOTE: A nice alternative to skiing all the way to the pipeline snowmobile trail is to turn around after reaching the cabin and ski back to Rte. 105, where you can find a spot to leave a car. If you are looking to leave a car the road is Mayhew Rd.

STATUS OF INDIVIDUAL SKI TOURS

Tour		Status
Tour A	MA Border to Route 9	Complete to Picnic Area
Tour B	Route 9 to Somerset Reservoir	Complete
Tour C	Somerset Res. to Kelley Stand Rd.	Complete
Tour D	Kelley Stnd. Rd.to Kendall F. Rd.	Complete
Tour E	Kendall Farm Road to Rte.11	Incomplete
Tour F	Rte. 11 to Landgrove	Complete
Tour G	Landgrove to Greendale	Complete
Tour H	Greendale to Healdville	Complete
Tour I	Healdville to Lake Ninevah	Complete
Tour J	Lake Ninevah to Tin Shanty	Complete
Tour K	Tin Shanty to Route 4	Complete
Tour L	Route 4 to Mt. Top	Complete
Tour M	Mountain Top to Blueberry Hill	Complete
Tour N	Blueberry Hill to Natural Turnpike	Complete
Tour O	Natural Turnpike to Lincoln Gap	Incomplete
Tour P	Lincoln Gap to Mad River Barn	Sugarbush to M.R.B. complete
Tour Q	Mad River Barn to CHNSC	Complete
Tour R	Camel's Hump to Bolton Valley	Complete, except river crossing
Tour S	Bolton Valley to Trapp Family L.	Complete
Tour T	Trapp Family Lodge to Edson Hill	Complete
Tour U	Edson Hill to Farm Resort	Complete
Tour V	Farm Resort to Route 15	Incomplete as of 1999
Tour W	Route 15 to Craftsbury	Complete
Tour X	Craftsbury to Lowell	Complete
Tour Y	Lowell Store to Jay Pass	Complete to Hazen's Notch XC
Tour Z	Jay Pass to Canadian Border	Incomplete

END-TO-END SECTION CHECK-OFF LIST

	Section	Date Skied
A	MA Border to Route 9	
B	Route 9 to Somerset Reservoir	
C	Somerset Res. to Kelley Stand Rd.	
D	Kelley Stnd. Rd.to Kendall F. Rd.	
E	Kendall Farm Road to Rte.11	
F	Rte. 11 to Landgrove	
G	Landgrove to Greendale	
H	Greendale to Healdville	
I	Healdville to Lake Ninevah	
J	Lake Ninevah to Tin Shanty	
K	Tin Shanty to Route 4	
L	Route 4 to Mt. Top	
M	Mountain Top to Blueberry Hill	
N	Blueberry Hill to Natural Turnpike	
O	Natural Turnpike to Lincoln Gap	
P	Lincoln Gap to Mad River Barn	
Q	Mad River Barn to CHNSC	
R	Camel's Hump to Bolton Valley	
S	Bolton Valley to Trapp Family L.	
T	Trapp Family Lodge to Edson Hill	
U	Edson Hill to Farm Resort	
V	Farm Resort to Route 15	
W	Route 15 to Craftsbury	
X	Craftsbury to Lowell	
Y	Lowell Store to Jay Pass	
Z	Jay Pass to Canadian Border	

NOTES